A MEASURE OF BELONGING

A MEASURE OF BELONGING

TWENTY-ONE WRITERS OF COLOR ON THE NEW AMERICAN SOUTH

EDITED *by* CINELLE BARNES

HUB CITY PRESS
SPARTANBURG, SC

BOOK DESIGN: Meg Reid, Kate McMullen
COVER ILLUSTRATION: John Mata
COPY EDITOR: Annie Crandell
PROOFREADERS: Jacquelyn Lancaster, Amanda L. Rosa, Kendall Owens
EDITOR PHOTO: Joshua Garcia

Library of Congress Cataloging-in-Publication Data

Barnes, Cinelle, editor.
A *measure of belonging : twenty-one writers of color on the new American South* / edited by Cinelle Barnes.
Spartanburg, SC : Hub City Press, [2020]
LCCN 2020029995 | ISBN 9781938235719 (trade paperback)
ISBN 9781938235719 (ebook)
Subjects: LCSH:
    American literature—Minority authors.
    Minorities—Literary collections.
    Southern States—Literary collections.
    Minorities—Southern States—Civilization.
Classification:
    LCC PS508.M54 M43 2020
    DDC 810.9/896075—dc23
LC record available at https://lccn.loc.gov/2020029995

Manufactured in the United States of America
First Edition

HUB CITY PRESS
200 Ezell Street
Spartanburg, SC 29306
864.577.9349 | www.hubcity.org

Contents

⊙ ⊙ ⊙

Introduction

Cinelle Barnes

TEN YEARS AGO, I FELL IN LOVE WITH A BOY FROM the Carolinas and followed him south, leaving the expansiveness of New York City for a small city on the Atlantic, a locale known for its food, its shadowed history, and its proud architecture. In spite of its ambitions and influence, the city still felt small to me in more ways than size.

Young and new to town, I nevertheless stepped out eager to receive all this new place would offer. On the night of my love's employee welcome dinner, I sat among wives of other transplants and wives of long-time staff. In the air-conditioned cafeteria where we escaped the August heat, wives fanned themselves with cloth napkins. I sweated in that room, tempted to dab my neck with my napkin. We had linens but ate off paper plates. I didn't know whether to relax or sit up straight. The manicured-casual way of dress didn't give any hints as to how I should behave. At this place of work, most people stayed until retirement. In fact, my new husband and I sat next to a sexagenarian couple who'd been with the employer for nearly a decade. I considered it a good sign: people loved to work there, they never left.

Right?

When the men got up to get drinks, the wife turned to me and stopped me mid-bite. "So, how do you like it here?" she said.

I told her that I loved the weather, the beaches, and historic downtown. But the part of me that had pursued a degree in journalism and literature—and was determined to practice what I was taught—told her the whole truth. Remembering how insular the city felt and how I stuck out without having to try, I said, "But there are definitely things I would change."

"Honey, nobody asked you to move here," the woman said. And that was all. She finished her meal, pushed her chair back, slapped her cloth napkin on the table, left, and never spoke to me again in the years that our husbands shared a place of work.

It was not that I wanted or needed to be asked to come somewhere or be a part of something. It was that I was told to my face, at a welcome dinner, by someone who could have been more than a stranger, that I was not, in fact, invited. The dismissal I felt that night would be felt again throughout the decade I've spent in the South.

I came of age in New York City, an undocumented immigrant from the Philippines. I had been adopted into Long Island; but when my citizenship petition fell through due to my age (too old to be naturalized through adoption yet too young to be on a work visa), I fell "out-of-status." Life became more challenging than what was promised by my adoptive mother. But still, a way was made for me. I was allowed an education from one of the city's sanctuary schools. From there, I had entry-level jobs and internships that launched me toward a career in journalism and the arts. I was given a hand up by people of various backgrounds and at different stations: lawyers and restaurant managers I worked for, relatives and friends who shared their resources, and teachers and mentors who offered wisdom and knowledge.

Their confidence (read: lack of mistrust or fear) in me permitted interactions and commissions I would not have otherwise had access to as someone deemed "illegal" by a government. So, you can imagine what they all said when I announced that I had met a boy and was moving south because, well, being undocumented had been so wearisome and worrisome and it was nice to love and be loved, to be and feel young.

They warned me: *There is nothing for you there. You're gonna turn right back around.*

Still, I moved.

In these ten years, I have published several essays and two books. I have gone on a cross-country book tour. I have spoken in front of audiences. This was not the life I foresaw for myself in the wake of the encounter at dinner. I had been convinced there were going to be unnatural yet obvious barriers to my mobility and achievement as a woman of color in the South. In these ten years, I have had interactions, been privy to conversations, and encountered institutions (tangible and not) that could have led me to believe what my former employers, friends, relatives, teachers, and mentors told me way back when. *There is nothing for you there. You're gonna turn right back around.*

I haven't turned back around. Instead, I've committed myself to making this place as big as it actually is. Because small is so ten years ago. Small is that woman who called me "Honey." Small is the South that saves its best smiles, best *hey y'alls*, and best resources to perpetuate a cultural homogeneity. And small are the books about this region that refuse to acknowledge and celebrate the voices and narratives of honey-me, honey-she, honey-he, honey-they, and honey-you.

And no, there is not nothing for me here. And there is not nothing for other people of color. There is not nothing for readers like you. There is this book, this anthology. There are the established and emerging writers herein who not only have, but share. While their stories and styles differ—perhaps more so than even I anticipated—a truth they share is that like most in their generation, they never bought into the lie that they did not belong here. These essayists know how to take up space and make space, in the way that only millennials and Gen-Xers know and zealously practice.

This is a collection of stories that say, "Honey, you come right here and sit up next to me." In Minda Honey's essay, she asks us to sit right up next to her on a stoop and listen to tales of generational hurt and hope. Andrew Carnegie medalist Kiese Laymon invites us to step into a recording studio and the mind of a Black man in Mississippi; Christena Cleveland asks us to hear conversations in academia and on Southeastern college sports. Joy Priest swings open her car door, takes us for a ride in her Cutty, turns up the volume on her radio, and makes us feel all the times she's felt young and all the times she's felt so old.

Here is *here*. When that woman said that nobody asked me to "come here," I decided that every one of my projects thereafter would be an invitation for other people of color to come, to be visible, and to thrive *here*. Each one of these essays, then, is an invitation to step into power and to empower, an RSVP to "Honey, I invite you to be here and tell me your story." My hope is that reading this book will activate you to make similar definitive choices wherever and whoever you are, so that, as Toni Jensen writes, this place would be a *we* rather than an it, that we all might feel a measure of belonging. ◉

A New Normal South:
Southern Cooking By Indian American Chefs Offers Refreshing Ways To Connect

Osayi Endolyn

I LOOK AROUND THE ROOM AT THE INAUGURAL Brown in the South dinner, and I shake my head in wonder. This event is the first in a new series, hosted at Meherwan Irani's Chai Pani restaurant in Decatur, Georgia. It centers chefs of Indian background who live and work in the American South: Irani, Vishwesh Bhatt of City Grocery Restaurant Group in Oxford, Nashville's Maneet Chauhan of Chauhan Ale and Masala House, cookbook author and founder of Atlanta's Third Space Asha Gomez, and Cheetie Kumar of Garland in Raleigh.

The six-course spread I enjoy with about 160 diners embraces and expands what Southern food means, like Kumar's deep-fried fish puppies served with chutneys and piccalilli tartar sauce. The boisterous crowd leaves me with a sense of awe, in part because the special evening feels strikingly normal.

At my table, I dine with white Atlanta farmers, a Kentuckian chef of Sri Lankan descent, a reporter of Indian heritage, and Southern-born African Americans who work in publishing and academia. This is the version of the South that I've wanted to be a part of since settling here, and to be truthful, the one I've found to be most elusive. The discrete parts have long been present, but don't always engage in the same space at the same time and under such joyous circumstances. The South these self-described "brown" chefs celebrate by their thematic collaboration wouldn't exist if they didn't stake a claim to it.

I am obsessed with one question all night: Why haven't I experienced this before?

I've spent more than a decade as a Southern resident. My initial move and continued presence here can be a topic of amusement for some friends and family, many of whom have limited, if memorable, experiences in this region. I still get ribbing from all sides—not just from the California-born. My maternal great-aunt, age eighty-seven, is a Louisiana native. From her Lake Charles home, she ponders how I ever left "out West." She briefly moved to the foothills of the San

Gabriel Mountains to be near her sister, and recounts, like the names of beloved children, all that I sacrificed by leaving: the year-round good weather, all that sun, the views, the range of cultures, and the diversity of cuisine. We have a routine:

"Do you miss it?" she asks, a gray-hued eyebrow arched.

"Not too much," I say.

"You *like* it here?" she presses, leaning toward me. 'Here' is anywhere in the South that is not the wide swath of the Los Angeles area.

"I do," I say.

"Hmph," she says, smiling, often settling back in her chair. "I surely did not see that coming."

My great-aunt is not the only one. Upon arriving in Atlanta in 2005, just about everyone I met expressed shock that I'd left LA. Years later, a Bay Area friend admitted surprise at the range of restaurants in Atlanta and Decatur. Two Cali buddies cut ties with the region because they didn't want to raise kids here— one practically fled North Carolina after the Marine Corps issued his honorable discharge; the other timed her departure so her forthcoming baby would have a California birth certificate, as she does. "I am not giving birth in Georgia," she swore to me over lunch.

I am proud to be a daughter of the West, but there's a lot of myth surrounding California. While it's still a promised land with many advantages, from public health to education, my home state has more challenges than some care to acknowledge. Los Angeles especially, a sponge for go-hard dreams, absorbs the sometimes-misguided hopes of the folks who flock there. Which is why the South continues to fascinate me. People bring hopes and dreams of all kinds here, too, even if that's a less-told story.

Newcomers to this country have a long history of merging their traditional dishes with local ingredients. Peanut stew, red rice, and gumbo echo the Senegalese mafe, jollof rice, and Nigerian okro soup enslaved cooks adapted upon arrival. Soleil Ho once wrote in *Taste* about being surprised banh mi in Vietnam didn't come on sliced white bread, as she was accustomed to in her family's rural Illinois home. Famously, early twentieth-century Greek families in Birmingham integrated their spices to the Southern larder, illustrated by the keftedes and souvlaki at present-day meat-and-three Johnny's Restaurant.

In Asha Gomez's award-winning cookbook *My Two Souths*, she offers a visually stunning guide that blends her native Kerala with this region. The Desi Diner, as the evening was nicknamed, pushed this conversation further. Irani made upma, a classic South Asian porridge-like dish, from grits stone-ground in Oxford. He drowned the upma in a broth of head-on shrimp and tomato patia for a piquant interpretation of shrimp and grits. Gomez served her spiced fried chicken on uttapam, akin to a johnny-cake. Bhatt's pork meatloaf came with a crispy root vegetable hash. The evening closed with his carrot halva bread pudding and Chauhan's hot chocolate spiked with garam masala and rose marshmallow. I blissfully sipped my mini mug, assured that the spice blend has a permanent place in my homemade cocoa recipe.

For people whose Southern identities have been inherited rather than forged, the question of belonging may feel overwrought. It's not. This distinction is easy to overlook when you have made your life in the place that you're from, or if you're not immediately interrogated for characteristics that set you apart from your neighbors. All of us have a role in building our own narratives. But if you never sat in your parents' laps and asked why they came to America, or had to justify to loved ones why you're moving so far away, it can be easy to understate the psychic shift required to make a place you're not from feel like home.

What the first Brown in the South dinner accomplished that struck me as revelatory was the open acceptance of an evolving identity by a broad range of diners, all at once. It certainly helped that the talent was world-class, all touting loyal followings; it helped that the room teemed with food industry insiders— all hungry for new conversations on the plate. Still, Brown in the South reminds us that this conversation isn't new. Opportunities to expand the definition of what the South "is" have always been available for consideration. Unfolding what the South can become is as much reconciliation and reeducation as it is adaptation. Chefs, historians, and writers still meet considerable obstacles when they seek tangible acknowledgement for the African roots of this country. We can celebrate the varied cultures that continue to shape the story we write for ourselves when we respect that the authorship has always been mixed.

What I want most from the Brown in the South dinner series is for it to one day be wholly unremarkable that a group of Indian American chefs would claim their Southern identity so boldly. I want the series—and events inspired by it—to eventually be welcomed as interesting but not groundbreaking. Because why wouldn't there be multiple ways of enjoying the myriad dishes on offer in this abundant region? I hope this is just the beginning of many similar beginnings. For all the noteworthy text on the Desi Diner menu, the words I was most excited about were "Vol i." ◉

Foreign and Domestic:
On Color, Comfort, and Crime in Miami

Jaswinder Bolina

WHEN I'M ON MY KNEES IN STONE MULCH AT ONE in the morning, my hands predictably raised above my head, my back to the three boys relieving me of my wallet, phone, and laptop bag, and one of them has a taser to my neck and another maybe has a gun, I can't help but marvel at how nice this neighborhood is. The two-story, mid-century condos in front of which I'm being mugged for the first time in my life are nestled around a courtyard's thicket of palms. They list for upwards of $250,000 though they're short on square footage and ripe for renovation, and the newer construction townhouses down the sidewalk to their right run upwards of $850,000 in the robust market of downtown Coral Gables. A canopy of royal poinciana glows Crayola green in white streetlight over the wide boulevard, and a row of Mercedes E classes and Range Rovers glitter black along the curb on an altogether easy Friday night. Even the distant bass rhythm of a band playing a street fest blocks away only deepens the calm. Location being the meat of good realty, I'm almost proud to say I can see my condo building from here.

With nothing left but my clothes and keys, the boys tell me to get up and don't turn around and run. "¡No mires y VETE!" they shout. I don't run. It seems silly to bother. I just walk quickly away, back towards the bustle of Restaurant Row, without any wobble in my legs, no racing heart, no tremor in my hands. An earlier bourbon with friends is fortifying me now, and I'm in sufficient enough shock to find all of this mostly irksome and oddly funny. To be mugged on such a quiet street in front of such rarified real estate after so many years walking home at far later hours in much lousier neighborhoods seems an especially vapid brand of irony. Somewhere Alanis Morissette is humming. It's also that the boys looked so discombobulated when I approached them waiting nervously between me and my half-another-block home. I nodded and offered, "Buenas," so casually that when they lunged, grabbed my shoulders, and spun me almost gracefully around, they seemed more startled by their actions than I was. It felt silly for everyone involved to allow a simple robbery to escalate into any kind of crime measured by degrees, so I kept repeating, "Okay. Está bien. Okay. Take it easy." And they did.

Later, there will be a cascade of adrenaline and anxiously asking the police to check on my wife to assure the boys haven't followed the address on my driver's license home. Later, there will be shudders of the near-miss, wondering if their taser actually worked, if that was an actual gun in the one kid's hand or just a stub of pipe. I'll second-guess myself for months thinking I should've turned around instead of carrying brazenly onward and saying hello to some boys leaning awkwardly there against a busted-up, out-of-place Hyundai at one in the morning. Later, the police will ask what they looked like, and I'll have to answer, "My height, skinny, black hair, brown skin, jeans and hoodies. Young, maybe eighteen or twenty." I'll learn they drove all over town looking for easy marks and, in their desperation, even robbed a couple of women of leftovers as the pair strolled home from a dinner out. Later still, a detective will tell me that a ping from Find My iPhone located these three boys somewhere up in Hialeah along with two other people, five undocumented bodies splitting a one-bedroom flophouse, but by the time Miami PD arrive, there is no evidence left there with which to charge anyone of anything.

Now, though, they've probably banged into their car and driven off, but I don't risk glancing backwards.

I go on retracing my steps to the bar, empty-handed and alone between luxury townhouses and luxury sedans on a cool night in February. Skinny, black hair, brown skin, jeans, and a hoodie. Maybe thirty-five or forty. If not for the white of my chin stubble, I might be mistaken for one of my muggers or at least mistaken for an older brother. This is the thing about living here; for the first time in my life, I really fit in. Unremarkable as rain in the rainy season, ordinary as poinciana, oleander, and palm, my skin, face, and body feel more at home in Miami than they've ever been allowed to feel anywhere else in this country. It's the brownness of South Florida, it's non-English, un-Americana, that I so adore about the place. In truth, I'm more a minority here than in other towns I've called home. Weeks pass between times I run into anyone descended of South Asia, but as far as most anyone can tell, I'm indistinguishably un-white, plainly part of the sunbaked one-of-us of Miami-Dade. Even the muggers here address me in Spanish.

Born and raised in Chicago and living for stretches in California, Michigan, Ohio, and Massachusetts, I've rarely felt so ordinary and accepted. In the predominantly white, Christian North, normalcy is defined and legislated by a self-satisfied majority such that the rest of us might be forgiven for feeling we're an invasive species resident in somebody else's country. Someone always comes along inquiring where I'm *really* from, the question always presented with an air of charitable curiosity as if my inquisitor should be congratulated for paying me any mind at all, as if this nation doesn't birth brown bodies. On the losing side of the Mason-Dixon, both, the definition and the legislators are less generous.

Miami, situated as it is south of the South, has no such trouble. Not even my name tangles a tongue here where hardly anybody speaks English only. I've been greeted in Italian, Arabic, Spanish, and Hindi, and in the unironically named Mint Leaf Indian Brasserie a few blocks from where I'm walking, a desi waiter once seemed downright tickled when I answered his English with Punjabi before he delivered my order to the kitchen staff in Spanish. This place is so contrary to what I know of America, I can't help but find it refreshing, and I'd like to elaborate further on the dynamics of race, language, culture, and class here, but I don't fully understand those dynamics. Miami is a mosh of immigrants and natives born of émigrés, refugees and retirees, hospitality and service workers, bankers and realtors, business moguls, drug moguls, celebrity moguls, and tourists upon tourists upon tourists. For all its diversity and cosmopolitanism, all its exploitative development and growth, all its gaudy luxury and catastrophic poverty, all of it inevitably doomed by certainties of climate change and rising seas, living here can feel like living in the hot, crowded, hyper-capitalist, multinational future. As if Miami is already the nation so many demographic, economic, and environmental studies predict the United States is becoming.

Of course, we can't escape the present. In November 2016, just a few months from tonight's misadventure, majorities here in Florida—and in the greater South in concert with those in a couple northern states I once called home—will lift a racist into the White House, his regressive platform built on a promise to wall the nation off from that impending fate. Those majorities fear my bad luck this evening will be our collective misfortune, that undocumented boys fleeing poverty and violence everywhere else are arriving here in droves to mug, rape, and murder America. Those majorities would rather villainous boys like these be left rotting in the streets of their own brown towns, but my town is their town, and the faces of the boys who mugged me had not one flicker of villainy in them. The only thing I remember is their bravado, the false front they barely mustered against whatever hunger had driven them to this quiet street on which I happened to be walking home. I'm not a victim of their malice. I'm a victim of their desperation, which is to say, my neighbor's misfortune becomes my own. Certainly, they should be found and prosecuted. Certainly, I'm scared and angry and violated. But their problems are also my problems. Hungry enough, frightened enough, hopeless enough, I might mug me too.

When the racist delivers his dark vision and his people deliver him to power in bleak November, I'll feel relieved to be living here among all these foreign bodies, even those of my muggers. Still, Miami is no perfect, post-racial paradise. Whatever its charms, it is home also to some of the most sinister inequalities of race, wealth, and opportunity on earth, and for all our global excesses, the ocean will drown it soon enough. No factor of income, no superficial artifact of birthplace or citizenship, no law or politician's pledge can keep us safe. This, too, is America. Whatever threat or violence awaits this nation in the years ahead, none of it lurks there because we permit diversity and difference to enter here. It lurks because we permit disparity and indifference, because we seek not to correct desperation and injustice but to insulate ourselves from them. If we have things that are worth taking, it's because we walk obliviously among those we leave wanting. We can detest, fear, and vilify whoever we want. We can abhor, imprison, and deport them. They will not leave us. They are us. In Miami, wherever you're coming from, wherever you think you're going, this is a fact that seems anxious to find you even when you are bothering no one on a quiet night, perfectly at home in so much lush and gorgeous weather. ◉

Face

Soniah Kamal

SHOULD I KISS HIS FACE? THIS IS A QUESTION NO mother should have to ask about her child, but there I was, staring at the face I'd delivered into my palms, and there was his opaque face staring back at me.

The first time I'd miscarried, I was a twenty-four-year-old newlywed and, because of a scheduling mix-up, I'd had to wait two days for a dilation and curretage, a surgical procedure in which my uterus would be scraped clean of the pregnancy. While I mourned the loss, I found it macabre and scary to be carrying death. Afterward, I was sad but mostly relieved. Since then, I'd had several very early onset miscarriages between two live births, but nothing so traumatic.

Now I was pregnant again.

After an uneventful first trimester, my husband and I announced that we were expecting our third child. Our seven-year-old son wanted a brother and our five-year-old daughter wanted a sister. They named their new sibling Lil' Mo; I have no idea why. They purchased infant socks from the Gap, size 0-3 months, crimson with white rubber on the soles, and placed them on the mantel like Christmas stockings. Lil' Mo's first 3D ultrasound photo, a dimpled knot, was pinned to the fridge with a pastel magnet that spelled B-A-B-Y.

A few days later, I dropped my kids at their elementary school and headed to the gym. We had recently moved to suburban Georgia for my husband's job. For immigrant me, Georgia was home to *Gone With the Wind*, Martin Luther King, Civil Rights, sweet tea, peaches, CNN, nothing more. In the absence of family and friends, exercise classes were my lifeline. After class, I headed home only to discover that I was bleeding.

I arrived at the OB-GYN's and readied myself for the inevitable devastation. But there was the shush-shush-shush of a beating heart and the OB-GYN proclaiming, "The baby is fine!"

Still, in the following weeks, heavier spells of bleeding would send me back several times. Each time I was assured that half of all women bled throughout their pregnancies. I picked out names: Sahara for a girl and Khyber for a boy.

One Thursday evening, when the bleeding sent me yet again to the emergency room, a compassionate nurse whispered that I was going to have a boy. The doctor added that he was moving so fast, he was going to come out playing soccer.

That night I had the worst bout of bleeding and as soon as Friday morning came, I rushed to my OB-GYN. I paced in the waiting room for two hours, even as scheduled patients requested the receptionist to send me in, before finally being taken to an exam room. Immediately, the OB-GYN began yelling at me even as she ran an ultrasound wand over my tummy. *You've just been checked the night before! You can't get constantly checked every single day just because you feel something is wrong! Nothing is wrong with your pregnancy! You are paranoid! Did you know how much you're costing the insurance company? Have insurance companies got nothing better to do than pay for you?*

Suddenly, she was still and silent.

I knew already. My baby—*Khyber*—was gone. Overnight.

The OB-GYN left so I could get out of the green gown and into my clothes. I met her in her office, which had a window looking out to a patch of flowers and a main road. Framed degree certificates and plaques with Bible verses hung on her wall. There was a plant on her desk. Her voice was soft as she told me that since the pregnancy was close to sixteen weeks, only specially qualified doctors could perform a late stage D&C. Since both the qualified doctors in our area happened to be Jewish, and because I'd miscarried on the Jewish New Year, they wouldn't be available until four days later. It didn't occur to me that they would have honored my request to be seen and, anyway, the doctor assured me that my progesterone was too high for a miscarriage to happen over the weekend, so she sent me home.

The last time I'd had a dead baby inside of me, I'd wanted to get it out of me as soon as possible. A baby implies life and it had been deeply distressing and macabre for me to have been carrying a dead child inside of me.

This time, I treasured a final weekend to hold in my baby. I kept cradling my belly and talking and sing-ing to him amidst tears. Friday and Saturday were a blur. I was unsure of how to tell my kids. I kissed the tiny crimson socks and thought of the story: "For sale: Baby shoes, never worn."

By Sunday evening, I started to have cramps and realized that not only was I miscarrying despite the OB-GYN's assurance that I would not, but that I was also in first stage labor.

I wish the OB-GYN had at the very least warned me that I might very well deliver my baby's face into my hands.

His face was no bigger than a kitchen cabinet knob. The outlines of his eyes, ears, nose, and mouth were clear. He looked like an alien out of *The X-Files* TV show.

Should I kiss him? The moment tested me as a mother like no other but there was no pass or fail, winning or losing. There was only the remains of my baby resting in my palms turned up prayer style and the sound of my own beating heart.

Finally, I held him to my heart before putting him in a sandwich bag, as the emergency room nurse instructed, so he could be sent for an autopsy. When I arrived at the hospital, a nurse said the autopsy results would take a few weeks. As I let go of the sandwich bag, an extreme weariness came over me. This was it. This was the end and now my baby's face would be cut up and perhaps put in formaldehyde to be studied. I felt sick. I was placed on a gurney in a small room and hooked up to IVs to monitor me for the next few hours.

There comes a time when even though you are crying, you are tearless. I just stared at the blank wall. A Christian chaplain came in and stood beside me. I grasped his hand tightly and he asked in a Southern accent, "Would you like to pray?"

I'd grown up in a secular Islam where people from all faiths in desperate need of miracles turned to each others' Gods.

"I'm Muslim," I said, "but prayers are prayers."

We prayed. He recited the Lord's Prayer, and I the Al-Fatiha, the prayer that begins the Quran; the one we recite at graves.

I couldn't stop sharing the story of my miscarriage with everyone. It was as if I had opened the gates to a taboo subject. Family, friends, strangers—everyone would share either their own miscarriage story or someone else's. It turned out that even my mother had miscarried before me.

And yet too many, including my husband, could not quite understand why I was so gutted. After all, I was told over and over again, I already had two kids. That I'd barely been sixteen weeks. I could have another one, as if babies are replaceable. I was told, "It wasn't a stillbirth. You weren't full term. It was just a fetus. Stop being so sad."

It left me upset and alone to have conditions put on grief.

One gray afternoon, after walking my kids back from the bus stop and serving them dinosaur-shaped chicken nuggets for lunch, I told them that instead of story time today, we would clean out their Spider-Man and Dora the Explorer backpacks. As they knelt on the rug in a patch of sunshine, their small fingers unzipping their school bags to expose canvas bellies full of crayons and scuffed books, I blurted out, "Lil' Mo is gone."

"Gone?" said my seven-year-old son.

"He died."

My son's best friend's father had passed away and so my son had an inkling of life after death: Darren's father was in heaven and heaven was a good place.

"So Lil' Mo's in heaven?" he said as his eyes filled up. "Like Darren's father?"

"Yes," I said. I knew that whether heaven really existed or not, it certainly belonged to little children confronted with mortality.

Over the next month, we began to recover—if recovery is the correct sum of time plus healing. My son put the ultrasound pictures in a photo album with pictures of his beloved dead guinea pigs. I took the crimson socks off the mantel and tucked them in the back of a drawer. Around the same time, I lost the contract for my debut novel. I'd always thought that book babies and human babies were equal creations, but now, having lost a book and Khyber back to back, never again would I think this was true. A book can be revived. A child cannot be replaced.

One day, I received a call from the hospital: What did I want to do with the remains?

As Muslims, we bury our dead. My husband called the local mosque to make arrangements. But he was informed that there could be no burial. In Islam, it is believed a soul enters the body at 120 days of gestation (about sixteen weeks) and since my miscarriage took place right around that time with no proof that a soul had indeed entered, Khyber could be considered only a soulless fetus.

Fresh grief engulfed me. I called the hospital's perinatal loss clinic: "Please don't throw him in the trash."

The kind woman told me that she'd seen the remains and she could tell he'd been a beautiful baby. I managed a thank you. She said the hospital would take him, with the remains of other such babies, for a collective cremation.

At first, thinking of a trip to the Holocaust Memorial Museum in Washington, I recoiled at the thought of my baby being one of many. But eventually, by day's end, I found comfort in the idea of a collective. That way, I told myself, Khyber would, at least, never be alone.

The cremated remains would be put in an urn and placed in a cemetery in Stone Mountain, Georgia. Until that moment Stone Mountain had been but a city where the KKK once had a stronghold, a city popular for a park with a laser show, a city with a cable car ascending to a manmade plateau offering a scenic view. *Does a city turn into a home when it rests your dead?*

We printed out directions to the cemetery in Stone Mountain where the ashes were buried. We drove in absolute silence through u-shaped headstones, many adorned with wreaths and Confederate soldier markers. My eyes searched for a small plot with a big urn shaded by an oak tree. Finally we found it. It was marked by a marble bench with a carved dove on it. My son had brought as an offering a miniature teddy bear I'd given him for Valentine's Day and my daughter a rose from our garden.

I sat on the bench with the carved dove.

I recited a prayer for my baby. I recited a prayer for all the babies. ☉

My Sixty-Five-Year-Old Roommate

Jennifer Hope Choi

NEWLY DISPATCHED FROM A RUM BAR'S HAPPY hour, my mother and I strolled along an oceanside square to await a sherbet sunset. It was Christmas Eve in South Florida, balmy and sun-drenched—a seasonal and thermal incongruence we'd enjoyed by then for three Decembers in a row. My mother parked herself on the pier's pavement, leaned against the railing, and with her back turned to the horizon, suddenly confessed: "My greatest wish is to live with someone I'm madly in love with."

A crowd had begun to form. Too-tanned, yam-colored couples decked out in Santa hats wove through children playing chase. I stood speechless. My parents had lived in California for twenty-seven years before their joyless marriage went kaput—an event that shocked no one and yet still elicited a painful and thorough family implosion. After they split, my mother began to wander. She had relocated plenty since first emigrating to America from South Korea in 1977, but never before with such acute vigor; by the time she got to Florida, over nine years she'd racked up eight moves across five states, with no foreseeable end to her newly adopted itinerance in sight. While hot-footing it job to job, she'd mentioned no suitors, no date nights. As she repeatedly put it whenever I inquired about her romantic life: "I'm not into that kind of thing." It seemed that at the pier, some buried part of her, summoned by daiquiris and our enchanting environs, had at last surfaced to insist otherwise.

Shutters clicked, and in the distance, a pirate ship traversed a melting sky. My mother slumped over, smiling faintly, her thought carrying off into the wind, already forgotten. Perhaps to her it had never been uttered at all.

To share a home with a love had not been a life goal of mine. I'd entertained the notion with boyfriends past, but the prospect only materialized as a matter of financial practicality. On my pauper-ish writer-bartender wages, I'd lived for seventeen years in New York City with a spate of concessions in trade for cheap rent. But after turning thirty, all the jerry-rigged setups had amounted to a depressing, Peter

Pan-ish portrait of adulthood. Acquiring an above-board apartment seemed plausible only through joint incomes—a highly inadvisable pretense to initiate cohabitation, but one I'd convinced myself could reap innumerable benefits. For example, the arrangement might unlock a new plane of trust with my partners, who needed much wrangling into our low-stakes commitments in the first place. Had I been in love with any of them? For a time. Madly so? Never long enough to sign a lease.

If anything, my greatest wish had been the opposite of my mother's: to live in a home I could call my own. An impossible task in New York, yet I couldn't muster the nerve to leave. Still, I pondered where else I might one day actualize my fantasy. Baltimore? Burlington? Either of the Portlands?

On my short list, the Deep South at no point sprang to mind. I'd recently returned from a writing fellowship in Georgia that constituted the loneliest stretch of my life. I resided in a house purportedly haunted by a specter or two, in a neighborhood once terrorized by a serial killer who'd targeted single women. I spent my time conducting research for a book on modern Korean cults; this included undercover visits to nearby heretical churches, where I posed as a spiritually lost person I believed to be parallel to my true identity. But the work rendered me a kind of specter too, in limbo between whoever I actually was and my guile-less simulacrum. It would have been easier being the latter, a believer, because when you trust in a higher power, there are always answers, absolutes. Instead, when I returned from the healing prayer circles and eight-hour revivals, to the house that creaked in the dead of the night, I lay awake in bed, undone. What was I doing? Where was I going? When I got there, would I still be alone?

Then I'd walk outside. The town itself, quaint at first, rattled me with its many anachronisms and contradictions: the overtly segregated nature of its residential sprawl; the brand-spanking-new, twenty-two-mile RiverWalk along the murky Chattahoochee—allegedly the site of the Civil War's final battle—whose waters were now outfitted with a man-made rapids course; and the third-wave coffee shop, housed in an old bank, serving espresso made from Brooklyn-roasted beans, just shouting distance from a behemoth oak known casually to some as "the lynching tree."

Photographs of such lynchings I'd seen at antique stores, stocked in faux patina farmhouse hutches beside Coca-Cola memorabilia, Sambo salt and pepper shakers, and blackface nutcrackers. There was the craft beer gastropub that served as a democratic call bank a short drive from a graveyard flecked with regularly replenished Confederate flags. I found people who looked like me scattered outside the city's center—owners of Asian markets and restaurants, their signage posted in the universal chinky font of small-town capitulations. But perhaps what startled me most were the unsolicited salutations, the immediate cordiality: smiles and hat tips from complete strangers, the politesse and adamant *ma'am*-ing.

In this place, the caricature, legacy, joy, and shame, of a history not yet fully escaped, had been put on display—which struck me as ghastly but honest. Further out, the landscape vibrated with a quiet violence. On long drives, I'd pass through pastoral expanses suspended in time: defunct mill towns, back-wood roads, acres puckered by tufts of cotton, soy fields whose verdant blades shuddered in the wind. After sundown, every few miles, a fluorescent cross illuminated an otherwise stark black night. Yet back in town, great energy, and funding, had been dispensed to make up for lost time, suggesting (as if it could be so easy): anyone can start over, especially here. When my fellowship ended, though, I was ready to leave.

Shortly after my Georgia stint, my mother called it quits on Florida. I flew down from New York to help with the move. She had never requested my assistance before, typically announced her latest change of address without much, if any, advance notice. Once she'd settled in, I was always the first to visit. Though the structural particulars changed, to me it appeared as if her many relocations had been occasioned through the magic of instant transposition; rearranged in slightly altered permutations, each house contained the same few objects of her life and post-divorce travels: the oil painting of the Seine she'd purchased from a street artist in Montmartre; a vibrant toucan drawn on a delicate white feather from Costa Rica; her license plates from the trail of states she'd left behind.

We stowed these keepsakes in boxes, loaded up the U-Haul, and then I watched her tiny frame fold into that fifteen-foot, dusted up truck, her doll-like hand waving out to me from the driver's side window. I climbed into her car, and before our two-woman caravan headed for the road, I locked the doors and wept. There had been no magic. She'd unceremoniously uprooted herself on so many occasions, alone, packing and unpacking and repacking her life, as if the next place might hold an answer to whatever she seemed to be seeking.

That night, we shared a bed at a Best Western Plus off Columbia's Two Notch Road. My mother, in recent years, had grown accustomed to falling asleep to true crime YouTube videos. She snored as the voice-over—a coroner's report detailing Jane Doe's freshly unearthed remains and embalmed severed head—blared from a miniature screen between our pillows.

The next morning, we drove past a Lizard's Thicket ("Country Cookin Makes Ya Good Lookin"), Maurice's BBQ Piggie Park, and a Bojangles. The first house we toured, my mother signed a lease on the spot.

. . .

Two months later, I bottomed out in Brooklyn. The hustle had lost its luster. I got hit by a livery cab while riding my bike, right outside my front door. I'd drained my savings. Buyers had been showing up unannounced at my apartment for insurance inspections. I kept bucking the inevitable until my cat got diagnosed with terminal heart disease—as if he had donated his little life to send me the undeniable message: *Lady, it's over*. I'd spent half my life in the city. Now it was time to leave.

So I sold most of my belongings, shoved whatever else could fit into a minivan rental, and drove away from the only place I'd ever truly called home. It was raining. Just a sprinkle at first on the Verrazano. My sick cat sat statue-still as we crossed into Jersey, sheets of torrential downpour slapping the windshield, Manhattan blurring in the distance. After white knuckling the wheel for thirteen hours, I pulled into an overgrown lawn. My new, sixty-five-year-old roommate greeted me. The diaphanous trim of her nightie fluttered like the gown of a ghost. Cicadas whirred a metallic chorus as bullfrogs heaved at the rim of a nearby pond. "Welcome to South Carolina!" my mother chirped. "Hee-ha! You're home."

To live with a parent as an adult is a strange gift. At a young age I'd surmised that my mother's matter-of-fact, often affectionless demeanor had concealed her deepest aspirations—a mode she'd adopted in order to hunker down in a dreary marriage, to feed and care for her family. The late-in-life vagabond spirit she'd come to embrace confirmed my assumptions but made her newly inscrutable. Who was she now?

Adjustments had to be made, on my part, to her habits. Over dinner, she didn't care for small talk, swallowed her kimchi and rice urgently, which summoned at meal completion a vociferous, lip-curling belch. She refused to shut the door while using the bathroom, so on my way to the kitchen I'd glimpse her zig-zagged body enthroned, straining over various concerns. Which is to say she hadn't changed much at all.

Sometimes, late at night, I shut off her true crime videos and lingered beside her, thinking about a story she'd once told me.

We had shared a bed when I was a baby. No matter how quietly she got up in the morning, I'd wake with a start and inconsolably cry and cry. She often wore her work clothes to bed for a stealthier exit, but I couldn't be fooled. Every morning, the heat of her figure vanished, and I lay awake, panicked that my mother might disappear from me forever. Then she returned and the universe realigned, my simple world made whole again.

In South Carolina, my book stayed unwritten. My cat died. But I did not feel lonely. We found my mother a Korean church, a Korean grocery, a Korean hairdresser. On jogs along this city's RiverWalk, I tipped my hat back to passersby and said hello. Soon, my mother got used to me, too. I cooked while she chatted about work (*This is how they* do *in the South,* she'd say with a cackle), or local headlines *(Did you hear about the Hilton Head woman? Tried to save her dog and got ate up by alligator!)*

Yes, the surrounding landscape still vibrated with a quiet violence. But one night at home, tipsy on wine, before nodding off to sleep, my mother offered another confession: "You left at seventeen. Exactly seventeen years later, you came back to me." She had that dreamy look, like that night on the pier. Then her thought, a wisp of a thing, floated off, already forgotten. Perhaps to her it had never been uttered at all. ◉

That's Not Actually True

Kiese Laymon

WHEN I GOT WORD FROM MY AGENT THAT I COULD record my audiobook, I assumed I'd record it in Memphis or Jackson. That's not actually true, because the first time I recorded anything for an audiobook, I recorded the prologue to Yrsa Daley-Ward's *Bone* in this tricked-out room of a Walking Dead house in the boonies of Oxford, Mississippi. Oxford, Mississippi is home.

That's not actually true.

The day that I leave my house to record my audio-book, three musty confederate soldiers are outside mowing my yard, laying my mulch, and smiling at each other. That's not actually true. The three workers were actually three white brothers from Mississippi, and the house I live in is not my house.

I only live in it.

Still, the white brothers who I want to call confederate soldiers look at me like I'm the only Black person living in my neighborhood. That's not actually true. They look at me like I have more money in checking than they have in savings. And that confuses me because I likely don't. It makes me question things I don't want to question about intellectual class, versus economic class, versus the belief in what's possible for niggers who record audiobooks in Mississippi.

The day that I leave my house to record my audiobook, I talk with one of the white brothers about how both of our mamas couldn't cook a lick, and how our grandmamas loved to make purple hull peas, cornbread, and squirrel and dumplings. The white brother tells me that meal is still his favorite meal. I tell him that I feel the same way. If we were characters on *This Is Us*, there would be music in the background telling viewers that the white brother and I are about to be buddies who text each other NBA statistics late at night. That's not actually true because though I'm at least seventy pounds more than the white brother, I haven't eaten meat in twenty-three years, and even when I did eat meat, seeing a squirrel floating in boiling perfectly seasoned water made me really sad. There's no music for that kind of reveal.

The white brother I shouldn't have called the

confederate soldier tells me he finished one semester of junior college and he enjoys working for the state. "I worked in law enforcement before that," he says. "Shit. I was the po-lice." This makes me question things I don't want to question about intellectual class, versus economic class, versus what's possible for niggers and white brothers I want to call Confederate soldiers in Mississippi.

This white brother, who I like a lot more than I'll admit to my Mama, asks what I'm up to today. I tell him that I'm going to teach. That's not actually true. My work today is recording my audiobook, but nothing in the world feels more awkward than telling a musty white brother who knows how to properly pronounce po-lice and coanbread, and mows the yard of the house I live in that I'll be in some studio recording an audiobook where I say the words "nigga" and "free" and "love" and "American" a lot, while he gets mustier and mustier for his weekly check.

The studio where I'm sent to record my audiobook is a few miles beyond the tallest confederate monument in town, beyond Oxford's square, and way off in a new sub-rural neighborhood that I didn't really know exists. I assume the houses are owned by other kinds of white folk who don't get musty for their monthly checks. That's not actually true.

But it kinda is. And it kinda isn't. And it kinda is.

The house where I will record my audiobook is owned by a white man from up north. He comes to the door in socks. He tells me his wife is at work and his kids are at school. I feel like I should take my shoes off, but I don't have on any socks and my feet are smothered in foot powder. Leaving white footprints all over this white man from up north's house would make a funny Black-ass story, but I have to come back the next day and I don't want him to fuck up the audio in my audiobook. So I keep my shoes on, limp my way upstairs to the studio, and think a lot about intellectual class, versus economic class, versus what's possible for niggers in Mississippi who don't record audiobooks for a living.

We start recording up in an attic he's turned into a studio. The white man in socks is an audio engineer. He has only ever recorded music from bands. The director for my audiobook is a white sister from New York. I will hear her voice on Skype. She will tell me when I read too fast. She will tell me when I read too slowly. She will say things that make me think we share politics. Though she will not say coanbread or po-lice, I will feel safe(r) in that studio with her on the other end of the Skype. I will think a lot about intellectual class, versus economic class versus what's possible for niggers and white sisters in Mississippi.

That's not actually true.

I will think about how every Black woman in my life has talked with me about their distrust, disgust, and disappointment with white women. "You have no idea how they really are," they tell me. Every time I say

I understand, they tell me, in different assemblages of language, that I really don't. Today, I wonder if I'm closer to understanding. I have far more disappointment, distrust, and disgust for Southern white brothers than for white men in socks from up north, or lefty white sisters from New York; because Southern white brothers inflict so much damage on the rest of us, and, though Southern white brothers don't know us Black folks, they could. Though they refuse to feel us, they can. Though they do not appreciate the peculiar grace with which we carry ourselves in the face of their investment in the American terror, they should. They know why we talk like we talk, eat like we eat, walk like we walk. Many of them talk, eat, and walk the same way. They know from whence we came, and what they've stolen from us, and instead of doing everything they can to fight our current billionaire Yankee Doodle Dandy President, who is equally adept at playing these Southern white folks for the gotdamn fools they insist on being while eating our suffering, these white brothers from the Deep South generally swallow our suffering whole and slowly drink their own suffering while insisting we be thankful to find work cleaning the creases of their faces, fingers, and plates.

That's not actually true.

I don't currently clean their faces, fingers, or plates for a living. I teach, write, and record audiobooks in Mississippi, and I consider my check a kind of Mississippi reparation.

That's not actually true.

The first day of recording, I will read sentences like: "You know white folks don't use no washcloths." Say phrases like: "If white Americans reckoned with their insatiable appetites for Black American sufferings..." I will use words like "cowardice," "motherfucker," "train," "nan," "feets," "preserves," "stars," and "star-nated." When I imagined these words, phrases, and sentences, I never imagined reading them in a sub-rural attic, a few feet from a white man from up north, across Skype from a white radical sister who teaches people how to read audiobooks, a few hours from sweet conversation with the white brother mowing my yard. I imagine a warm, wet kind of Mississippi Blackness behind me, ahead of me, all around the sides of me. I imagine that warm, wet kind of Mississippi Blackness because it is here and it is there, in spite and because of, all of the sweet trifling white folks we have to deal with when doing our work for the day.

That's not actually true.

My agent, who loves me like a blood, is a white brother. My editor, who I dreamed of collaborating with for years, is a white sister. The head of the corporation that owns my publisher is likely a white man from up north. So I've been thinking long, hard, soft, and silly about the politics of making Black Southern art objects for Black Southerners when few, if any actual Black folks, or actual Southerners, are inherently built into the publishing process. And I've been thinking longer, harder, softer and sillier about how to craft a Black Southern self or subjectivity surrounded by so many layers and layers and layers of whiteness, and non-Southernness.

That's not actually true.

I've been thinking about Black loneliness, about having children in my forties, about buying jeans that make my big-ass thighs look less like big-ass thighs.

As I drive home from my first audiobook session, I'm thinking about the white brother I wanted to call a confederate soldier and how there's a 75 percent chance he voted for Trump, which means there's a 75 percent chance he thinks my trans and gender-non-conforming fam should be discriminated against, and thinks Muslims and Mexicans should suffer, and he supports giving massive tax breaks to tax brackets he will never ever occupy. I'm thinking about how most people treated like niggers in Mississippi do not record audiobooks. They do not live in homes owned by universities. Most people treated like niggers in Mississippi do not have any expectations of the white folk who believe in them.

That's what scares me most today.

I have little expectation that white men I want to call confederate soldiers will stop fighting for the confederacy, but I really want them to. I really want them to reconsider who they are, what they've done to us, what they've done to their insides, what traditions we share. I know, though they refuse to accept it, our relationship is a blood, Black, and cultural relationship and we can be better. I know one day white Southerners will fight next to Black, Indigenous, and Latinx Southerners for a country and region invested in well-funded public education, the best health care for all in the world, robust unions, and formalized racial reconciliation that redresses the labor, second chances, and healthy chances brutally stolen from us. I know that one day soon white Southerners will stop letting folks who have no love for them, or us, play them for the violent, pitiful fools.

That's not actually true.

White folk, regardless of region, are going to do what white folk do. That might be the most shown but not told lesson in American history. What are we going to do while they do what they've always done? How are we going to get better at loving, organizing, and caring for one another in the face of white folk who believe in Mexican, Muslim, and Black ghosts that never actually haunt them?

Weeks after I finish my audiobook, I will be interviewed on NPR by a much older white man from up north. I will imagine him sliding around his office in his socks. Near the end of our interview, he will ask why I still talk to my mother. I will say, "Oh my god." Then I will tell him the question should be why do we still talk to y'all when, Northern or Southern, y'all refuse to critically engage with your investment in your belief that niggers ain't shit. I will answer before the older white man from up north can answer and say, "If y'all ever paid us what we worked for, we wouldn't talk to y'all. You know that right? But we ain't got no money so we talk to y'all. And we hope it makes our checks bigger."

That's not actually true.

I said, "Oh my god." And I told the white man from up north that I loved my mama. My mama would hear the interview a few days later and she would tell me she was proud of me for telling the truth. That's not actually true. Mama was proud of me because I lied to the old northern white man with Black bombastic grace, style, and precision, as niggers down South have been trained to do when talking to white Southern sisters, white Southern brothers, white Southern gender-queer people, northern whites, and white folk worldwide since way before Grandmama and them wore short pants. And that is actually true. ◉

Duos

Devi Laskar

I'M TASKED WITH NEGOTIATING, ON THE PAGE, how I have managed to be a Southerner while simultaneously being a person of color. I'm not sure that I have been able to be both—I think there have been moments where I have felt safe enough to insist that I was a Southerner as a person of color. These moments were usually in the company of friends or family. Typically, though, when I am in the South, strangers either welcome me to the country of my birth or tell me to go home. Post-2016, I feel I am a trespasser— and I combat this by making certain that I carry two valid forms of identification with me wherever I go.

One of the reasons I wrote *The Atlas of Reds and Blues* was to explore these very topics: What constitutes being a Southerner? What constitutes being an American? I was born and raised in North Carolina. Prior to moving out west, I'd spent sixteen years in Georgia. The first time I wrote the story that became my debut novel, it was 2004. I still lived in an Atlanta suburb—and I wrote about a fictional Atlanta neighborhood and this family's place in it.

I can't imagine *The Atlas of Reds and Blues* in a different location—the South, especially North Carolina, Georgia, and Florida, figure prominently in the novel. In fact, place and how my main character interacts with her surroundings is the crux of my book. The setting is as much a main character as Mother, the narrator.

I am no longer a Southerner by physical location these days. I left Georgia in 2012, and not by choice. It is true that I reimagined and rewrote the novel while living in California. Still, I relied on my lifetime's experiences as an often-unwelcome Southerner to complete this book. It is place that grounds the reader and it is place that grounds the writer as well.

Here is where I segue to the recent past before I can restart my thoughts through a darker lens. In 2010, my husband was targeted by his former employer in Georgia. One Monday morning, the state police raided our suburban Atlanta home and seized many of our things, including my laptop. All of the police that day wore Kevlar and were armed with assault rifles. One of them pointed his weapon at me when I first returned home after taking my children to school. By the time the police took everything out of my house, I was sitting at a coffee shop two miles away, calling an attorney. The police said I could stay and watch them remove my belongings but only if I agreed to be placed in handcuffs. I opted out. I learned hours later, after they trashed my house and left, that they had seized our computers and our passports (which they did not have a warrant for). It took several days for our attorney to have our passports returned.

The two sentences we heard repeatedly for six and a half years: *You must have done something wrong. You should have known better.* We had so many retorts ready at the lips, but no one really cared to hear our answers. Although a state judge in Georgia in 2016 dismissed all of the charges levied against my husband years before, to this day most of our belongings have not yet been returned. This includes my laptop.

All this to say that I lost most of my work and I had to start over. Begin again.

I want to say that I'm an expert in beginning again. I did every day as I grew up; I do it still when I visit family. All of my formative years were spent in North Carolina—except for the year my dad did his sabbatical in West Germany (yes I'm that old; I remember a time when there were two countries named Germany) when I turned eight, and the many summers I spent in

India visiting family and friends. I was raised in the South, but inside my parents' home was India, their version of West Bengal: food, music, language, culture. This was their haven from the wide, white world around them. In the mornings I would go to school and be American. Once I came home from school and in the hours until bedtime, it was the bustle of Kolkata as best as my mother could envision it. The TV blared from the den; the diced vegetables rested in a plastic colander in the sink. Whole buffalo carp thawed in a melamine bowl and the smell of ground spices permeated the air. My first jobs were to change from my mother-approved Indian outfit into "home clothes," as she called it, wash my hands, eat a salty Indian snack, and start my homework. Although the voices on TV were speaking English (usually Phil Donahue or, later, Oprah), we only spoke Bengali to each other at home. After dinner, my father would play only mournful Bengali music on the Eight-Track. For many years my mother won out on our frequent battles about clothes, and I had to wear Indian outfits to school—ones she brought back from the subcontinent.

Although my mother was working on a master's degree in English when she got married and moved to the United States, there was little she could do with her knowledge of British English in Chapel Hill. Outside our home, she often stared, perplexed, at strangers, their Southern accents incomprehensible to her multilingual ear. She often muttered in Bengali, "I don't understand." Typically, I rescued her—interpreted, translated, made a small joke to ease the tension. Typically, these interactions were with older white women, at the pharmacy or the Food Lion, at Hancock Fabrics or the North Carolina National Bank. After I stepped in, the older ladies stopped looking at her and focused their gaze on me. Their scrutiny, their assumptions, made me feel small and big simultaneously; my otherness was enlarged, as if they were staring at me through a magnifying glass.

"You're from here? You don't look like you're from here," these stranger ladies often said. Once at the grocery store, one of these women came within inches of my body and touched my hair. Another time, one reached over and fingered the beadwork at the hem of the kurti top my mom had made me change into before leaving the house. This was code— you aren't white. Often, I smiled. I learned later that is what primates do when threatened: grin. Often, I took out my Southern accent and applied it so they could understand what I was saying without feeling the direct sting of my contempt. Few things are worse than having to fake your way through a conversation you didn't want to have with a woman that if you're rude to just then, you would no doubt run into six times a day for the next two years.

At home, my mother was more clearly in charge when she wanted to be. She corrected me every time I accidentally switched into English. The few phone calls that came from India never lasted very long—the script was the same. Our parents reassuring their closest relatives our health was fine, reassuring them we in America hadn't become "American"—loud-mouthed, disrespectful, disdainful of family—in short, all of the things our relatives saw on old soap operas (think *Guiding Light* and *The Bold and The Beautiful*) that were sometimes broadcast on a communal neighborhood TV a few doors down from their Kolkata homes.

My parents were typical immigrants. Every moment in the present was placed on hold so that it could be shared via letter or infrequent phone call—home to India. Every extra dollar was stowed toward the tickets home and toward future purchases for family who lived eight thousand miles away. They spoke to each other in Bengali and often reminisced about their large families and their childhoods in India. Everything was different in America, and they clung fiercely to their memories. We were alone in the new world.

"Do whatever you need to do when you are outside," my father said to me once when I was in the eighth grade. "But at home, we are back in our native place."

No one in our extended family thought the migration to America and then to the South was a permanent one. They came in 1964, a year after marriage, to California where my father was a visiting guest professor. The following year, he received an offer from the University of North Carolina. They took it, thinking they'd stay for a few years and then go back to India. I came along the following year, then my sibling came along a few years after that. Although they talked about it frequently, my parents were clearly stating that these were merely dreams of returning home; that our reality was that we weren't leaving America.

I grew up, became a newspaper reporter, and moved around state to state for my jobs and for graduate school. Beginning again. Each new place brought with it new encounters with strangers, and unfortunately, new voices asking familiar questions: *Where are you from? No, really. Where are you really from?* Georgia. Florida. Illinois. Hawaii. New York. Georgia again. Each visit to my parents a not-so-subtle reminder that I was a Bengali girl, that I had a large and loving family thousands of miles away.

It was this dual existence that informed my writing of my debut novel, and most likely informed my desire to grow up and become a poet and writer. As difficult as it was at times, I wouldn't trade my upbringing for anything. It formed who I am. ◉

I Feel Most Southern in the Hip-Hop of my Adolescence:
On Black Southern Mobility, Intra-regionality & Internalized Misogyny

Joy Priest

MY SOUTHERNNESS WAS SEEDED BY THE MATRI-
archs on my father's side, Black women who came up
from Alabama sharecropping fields in the twentieth
century to do "day work"—the language a euphe-
mism for taking care of white families, a pentimento
of the plantation schedule. In my own lifetime, I found
affirmation of my Southern identity in the music of
my adolescence, where I spent a lot of time in cars.
In the aughts, Kentucky didn't have a definitive sound
on mainstream radio, but Black Kentuckians heard
our experiences in Southern hip-hop no matter which
state it came out of—Georgia, Louisiana, Texas,
Mississippi, Alabama, North Carolina, Tennessee,

Florida, Virginia. We didn't feel Southern because we were listening to Southern rap. We felt Southern rap because the tempo matched the cadence of our lives and kept a record of the peripheral cultures that shaped our language and movement.

1999. "Back that A** Up," Juvenile feat. Mannie Fresh & Lil' Wayne | "I Need a Hot Girl," Hot Boys *New Orleans*

The seminal, intra-regional anthem for the Black South came down at the end of the twentieth century. There wasn't a party "Back That A** Up" failed to play at up through my exit from high school in 2007. A hood cult classic like Mr. Bigg's "Trial Time." To know every single word, affect, ad-lib was a mark of belonging.

It was at a grown folks' house party. It was at a school dance. A family reunion, barbecue. It was at the car wash, corner store. Sundays at Cox Park. From a car radio, sound distorted as it passed from right ear to left, or a chance snippet at the stoplight. On Broadway after school, where the old skools swerved like one slow-moving, shimmering river, mimicking the Ohio running parallel nine blocks away. It was on 106 & Park, BET Uncut, Video Countdown, Cita's World, Hits from the Streets, Rap City. It was practicing in front of the mirror. It was when we still called it "poppin." In pantsuits, capris, sundresses, air-brushed t-shirts or spaghetti straps, basketball & booty shorts. Hair store flip-flops or fresh, white Forces. Gold nameplates and jumbo hoop earrings airborne in the slow-motion music of our millennial turn.

It was at the F.Y.E. music store on Dixie Hwy in Louisville—our city twinned with New Orleans by the fleur-de-lis. It was in a bin that held piles of compact discs, a medium so delicate and ephemeral we kept cotton pads and light-abrasive polishing solutions in the medicine cabinet. In one bin, the CD covers featured the late-nineties Ca$h Money Records D.I.Y. graphics: diamond-encrusted block letters, old skools, and cash raining down to douse flames circling Lil Wayne or Juvenile or B.G. or Turk. The flames were always the most prominent feature. The rapper was depicted in the underworld—it was easy to internalize the evil and immorality projected onto us by residents from the 'good' side of town—in the ghetto as purgatory, necessarily a wellspring of creativity. We invented strategies to get by, made a way out of no way. The alchemical rapper demonstrated his three-pronged strategy for keeping the heat under control—money, mobility, ice.

It wasn't just the cover designs that held fire, but the titles too: *The Block is Hot, 400 Degreez.* "I need a hot girl," sang The Hot Boys. The heat was everywhere in the Black enclaves of the lower United States:

kitchen fires and hood summers; blocks saturated with police; a specific kind of girl who usually didn't get the gift of serenade. So, when Mannie Fresh sung his ode to hoodrats, we celebrated this newfound exclusivity by blessing someone who shared our claustrophobic swelter with a dance.

2000. *Stankonia*, Outkast | "Danger," Mystikal prod. by Neptunes | *Atlanta, New Orleans, Virginia Beach*

In Old Louisville—a well-preserved historic district downtown, populated exclusively by Victorian houses—Ninth Street branches off from Seventh Street like an empty aqueduct. From there it begins its journey northwest toward the West End (Somebody said: "the West End the Best End!"). By the time Ninth Street makes it to Broadway—the city's major downtown thoroughfare—it has become a border with enough narrative resonance in our city to have earned a nickname: The Berlin Wall. Called such because it separates the West End economically, politically, visually, and psychically, the Ninth Street Divide is a common phrase uttered to tourists by downtown bartenders as a boundary not to venture beyond.

Historically, it served as a divide between urban renewal "projects" and the business district. Currently, it corrals Black Louisvillians within thirty or so blocks, effectively cut off from the rest of the city, its sit-down restaurants and hospitals, movie theaters and stores. Thirty percent of West End residents do not own a vehicle. But the bus route will eventually get you to work on the other side of town, and on foot you can get to church or the liquor store, depending on what kind of spirit you are trying to catch—fire in your belly or fire on your head.

In the first year of the new century, your slightly older, teenage uncle has a 1983 Z28 Camaro, T-top. It's a bucket, but you want the same car when you get older. There's a detaching face CD player and some rattle in the trunk, but the power windows won't come down, and it's burning up in the early morning heat wave. At every pothole or railroad track, the radio cuts out. There's a short in the wiring, but his guy says it's not worth the cost to fix it, so he resorts to the usual: banging on the dashboard until it cuts back in.

2001. "Raise Up," Petey Pablo, produced by Timbaland | *Greenville, Norfolk*

2002. *Watermelon, Chicken & Gritz*, Nappy Roots *Choppa Style*, Choppa | *Bowling Green, New Orleans*

At the end of every week, we started in early with pleas to convince our parents to let us go to Saturday Skate at Champs roller rink, located on the ominously curvy Manslick Road, where the working-class white and Black sides of town converged. It was, each time, a difficult convincing, considering the night always ended prematurely with a fistfight or a skate opening someone's scalp. But somehow, we managed to arrive under the glow-in-the-dark purple lights with money-in-hand for speed skates and Surge soda.

There was always a favorite cut that got everyone to the floor, when the rink reached capacity and speed skates became pointless inside the slow-turning mass. Petey Pablo was talking about a place none of us had thought about before, but when *"rep yo city!"* refrained from the rink speakers—in that gravel-crunch voice that held the church and the liquor store—we raised up.

Maybe North Carolina hated this song. Maybe the "big city" Black folks in Charlotte were embarrassed by that country shit, the way "big city" Black folks in Louisville were embarrassed by the first, mainstream Kentucky rap group that would debut the next year with *Watermelon, Chicken & Gritz*—a corny misrepresentation too public to defend. When they sang about their newfound contentment with lifelong poverty, in an over-pronounced twang, we weren't trying to hear that. Being poor definitely still mattered to us and the struggle wasn't something we were in a place to look back on, as teenagers, and celebrate. Still, these songs of representation at the beginning of the millennium portended a come up for those of us living in American obscurity.

As we transitioned into the Crunk era, reppin' your

city became reppin' your set. Our spaces shrunk and our divides multiplied beyond North-South or poor Black-poor white. The block got hotter and our square radius became even more constricted.

In the meantime, back at the rink, we kissed our teeth at the boys and skated onto the floor to the "ooawwwww" and *wop wop* drums that signaled the start of "Choppa Style." In that moment, wasn't none of us trying to parse our circumstances with intellect. We were trying to feel it. Trying to turn so many revolutions around that rink that we couldn't feel the heat anymore for the wind. We knew what difference a breeze made inside a cage, how much mobility mattered inside a loop you couldn't figure out how to exit.

2003. "Never Scared," Bone Crusher | "24s," T.I. | "Like a Pimp," David Banner | "Ridin' Spinners," Three 6 Mafia | *Gangsta Musik*, Boosie & Webbie *Atlanta, Baton Rouge, Jackson, Memphis, New Orleans*

After roller skates, but before rims, there were the wheels on the bus. School bus. City bus. For a few hours a day, passing between the enclosure of our neighborhood and the enclosure of a school building, you got to be rogue and alone. Or, at least you didn't have to talk to nobody. Inside the private experience of the Walkman, the CD revolved silently. Some songs you spun so much the CD began to skip...*swer-swer-swer-swer-swerve on 'em.* Or, after a while, the wire to the headphones would short, at which point you'd have to find the spot in the wire and pinch it just right for the duration of the ride lest your music sound distorted and distant, like someone had thrown a low pass filter on it. Once the wire shorted, you had to find someone to let you hold $10, and then you had to walk down to that Walgreens to get new earphones. The Walgreens past your ex-best friend's house, where, after he had bought you a large McDonald's fry, her older brother lured you to his room under the guise of music and tried to get you to let him lick you between your legs. You could man up and go down to Walgreens, vulnerable on foot or, the next day, you could ride in the 6 a.m. silence with the whole, deadening school day ready to come down on you.

2004. *Crime Mob*, Crime Mob | *Tha Carter*, Lil Wayne | *Urban Legend*, T.I. | *Straight Outta Cashville*, Young Buck | *Atlanta, Nashville, New Orleans*

Some of us left in the furnaces of steamboats. Some left as porters on the train. Some stayed. Some migrated North, but not far enough. If you landed in Kentucky, say, from Alabama, you might have thought of it as the North before you got there, but realized it was still Dixie once you arrived. Everywhere in America, Dixie. Everywhere a running history of bondage beneath the surface of society, peeking out.

In the nineteenth century, rather than a plantation

structure, the Louisville economy was organized around a bondsman system—an ironic mobility for Black folks who were "rented out" to various proprietors around the city for task-based jobs, rather than confined to an estate, physically-speaking. In the mid-twentieth century, this class structure remained in place, but mobility became increasingly more restricted after 24/7 electric streetcar service ended in 1948. As Black folks bought homes, white flight commenced in the West End, and the Ninth Street Divide became a defining reality.

To have your own car meant everything. It was a symbol of mobility and success in a southern city that did not have a mass public transportation system or an Amtrak rail to ride out of state—just a fraught inner-city bus line to get you downtown to your restaurant job or assembly line. Fast-forward to the aughts and car culture was a thriving, Black Southern art genre, a canvas for one's personality and style. This was one of the peripheral cultures that Southern rap preserved for us, alongside our dance anthems and idioms, gold grill fronts, lunch table beats and internalized misogynoir.

The fall of her sophomore year, a girl drives her 1988 Cutlass Supreme Classic to school with just a permit (a perfectly acceptable thing to do as a 15-year-old in Kentucky). Her father's co-worker at Hytec Cutting Services has sold it to her for a charitable $500.

When she drives up to Central High Magnet Career Academy—a fancy name that belies the poor state of Muhammad Ali's historically-Black alma mater—she has the respect of men. They begin to invite her on exclusive dips to practice formations for "cruising" at the park or on Derby. In the era of Crime Mob, when even the dudes rap Princess' and Diamond's verses, it is acceptable to have a girl in your crew. And, as a girl, if you have something that interests boys besides your body, it saves you a lot of trouble.

The body of her car is in mint condition. Oxblood drip. 307 V8. At post-9/11 gas prices, her entire Sonic Drive-In paycheck starts going to gas. It doesn't matter, as long as she can take herself wherever she wants to go and leave whenever she wants to leave, as long as she isn't the girl Young Buck raps about in "Shorty Wanna Ride," trapped in some dude's fantasy, just another commodity, or feature of his car.

2005. *Thug Motivation 101*, Young Jeezy
Savage Life, Webbie | *Who is Mike Jones?* Mike Jones
The People's Champ, Paul Wall | *Tha Carter II*
Lil Wayne | *The Sound of Revenge*, Chamillionaire |
Atlanta, Baton Rouge, Houston, New Orleans

2005 was the definitive year. We stayed with a burnt copy of *Thug Motivation 101* on repeat and by now some of us had managed to get two 12s in the trunk with whatever was left over from our busboy tips and dime bag sales after helping out at home. It was the year Mike Jones gave out his number on record, the year we rapped along to "Flossin" at the top of our lungs out the window. It was the year Chamillionaire gave us an anthem for racial profiling, and Webbie spit every car known to man in a 16. It was the year even a white boy came with that heat on "Sittin Sidewayz," "Still Tippin," and "Drive Slow," and had the internet going nuts before most of us even had the internet.

"Let's meet up on 11th street tonight," Man-Man yells out his window at the Marathon gas station before we get tight out of the parking lot and down 18th street: our after-school tradition. The heat built up over the course of a day inside our air condition-less school building.

Sometimes we'd drive in a formation. We had the choreography down because we rode together a lot, went on dips out on the empty, old roads. We knew one another's cars down to the transmission, and how a certain person drove, their idiosyncrasies and inclinations toward stupidity and recklessness. We were made lion-hearted by our mobility.

We were also made more vulnerable. Having a car meant more encounters with the police.

. . .

That year a girl gets her first reckless driving charge for burning rubber as she turns from 18th onto Broadway, and, just in case her high yellow ass is still confused about how white people and authority figures see her after 12 years in public school institutions, the officer makes sure to check "Black female" on the citation.

2006-2007. *King*, T.I. | *Port of Miami*, Rick Ross *Thug Motivation 102: The Inspiration*, Young Jeezy *Dedication 2*, Lil Wayne | *Underground Kingz*, UGK "Throw Some Ds," Rich Boy | "Shoulder Lean," Young Dro | *Atlanta, East Texas, New Orleans, Miami, Mobile*

By 2006, we were in an era of sequels. The murder count in our city rose, and loss became so mundane as to be anti-climactic, sublimating our joy and suspicions of an elsewhere. Some encounters lasted longer than others. Sometimes we were each pulled out of our cars and questioned individually. Sometimes we asserted our rights—"no you may not search my car"—but most of the time we had none. Sometimes they made us leave our means of transport behind. Sometimes we chose to leave it, voluntarily, while the whip was still in motion. A ritual for our ghosts to ride.

One day a girl walks out of the school building to find her parking spot empty. Weeks later, her

Cutty is found in Victory Park, a Crip-heavy block in Louisville's California neighborhood. Unwilling to walk in and retrieve it, she has to wait for it to be towed.

A month later, on her way home from the impound lot, the rods are knocking and the motor running hot, turning off at every light she comes to. Some young kids on a joy ride dogged it. Eventually, it locks up, right where 18th turns into Dixie Hwy— the engine gone quiet, the music persisting into the warm night. She sends word to one of her boys to come get her and he comes.

Bonus Track: New American South.
Rapsody | Missy Elliott | Megan Thee Stallion Janelle Monae | Diamond & Princess | City Girls | Trina | Left Eye | Lizzo | Big Freedia | CHIKA Mulatto | Jackie O Khia | La Chat | Gangsta Boo Chyna Whyte | Mia X

Some fifteen years later, I look back on the soundtrack of my teenage angst and realize that women rappers—while tucked into a verse here and there in our CD cases and LimeWire files—were not as prolific or celebrated in the rap we gloried in as the men. I was trying to survive my girlhood, not make it conspicuous via loud recitation.

If this was the record of our lives and, if the voices

of women rappers were non-existent or accessory, then so were ours, so were we. What this archive reveals is that, when we were young, what started as a weak solidarity between boys and girls advanced to a game of chase, the psychology of the hunt, and graduated to expectations of sexual favors and harassment as a measure of one's manhood. In this progression, all association with femininity became dangerous; to distance yourself from the feminine in you was a survival strategy.

However, Southern women make legible a whole periphery of possibilities. What kind of mobility would they have offered to a 16-year-old Black girl wanting out of a male-oriented cypher? What vehicle?

Self-possession: "I remember when hot girls and hot boys needed one another," read a recent tweet in response to Megan Thee Stallion's 2019 Hot Girl Summer campaign. The tweet was a clever reference to the 504 Boyz hit twenty years earlier. A lament, but a necessary one. Hot girls and hot boys definitely need one another, but this togetherness requires a revisioning: a solidarity in which we recognize and honor the full humanity of one another, and ourselves. If we continue to look at women/femmes as potentially exploitable, we are only mobilizing toward more airless purgatories.

Mental mobility: Last year, Rapsody put out a 16-track album—each track eponymously citing a Black woman, a small liberation of the archive. And, a few years before, on Kendrick Lamar's 2015 *To Pimp a Butterfly*, she dropped her anti-white supremacist ethos. For her language and thought are the currents on which we take flight. ◉

Suddenly, an Island Girl

M. Evelina Galang

WADING INTO THE OCEAN, I FLOATED ON MY BACK. Closed my eyes. Pointed my toes to the sun. I heard only waves. But once I placed my feet on the seafloor, I heard people talking. I didn't understand everything, but for me, this was comforting.

In Miami, you can slip into the Atlantic and hear a polyglot of languages. Russian, French, Spanish, Arabic, Hindi, Tagalog.

Yesterday, I was at the beach with my friend, Patty, a Colombiana from New Jersey. We glided through the water, exchanging tsismis. I felt a splash, and turning, saw a set of five-year-old twins with matching pixie smiles. They wore bright pink swimsuits that had MERMAID AT HEART scrawled in glitter across their small torsos. They flexed the plastic floaties wrapped around their arms.

"Where are your floaties?" asked one of them.

"I don't need them," I answered.

"Why not?" asked the other.

Each one was missing teeth. On their ears were shiny earrings.

"Because I'm an adult," I answered.

"Adults don't need much in the ocean," said the one with red floaties. "Just a swimsuit, and sunglasses."

"Sometimes you can see their bellies too," said the thinner-faced twin.

"Your skin is darker," said red floaties. She touched my arm. "Ours is lighter."

"Yes, that's true," I said. They spun around me like colorful koi fish.

"Hers is lighter," said the thin-faced one, pointing to Patty.

"What?" said my friend. "I'm lighter? No."

It was as if the twins had surfaced from the bottom of the Atlantic, sea angels guiding us to warmer waters. They spoke without censors, without fear, playing off each other in one continuous stream of words.

"Did you know there's no such thing as God?" asked red floaties. "He's a fake."

"Yeah, a fake."

"Who told you that?" Patty asked.

"Our mami. She says our abuela talks crazy and there is no heaven."

"Plus, she only speaks Spanish," said the thin-faced one.

"Who only speaks Spanish?"

"Abuela. We speak two languages."

"Oh yeah?" I asked.

"Spanish and English."

There, at the edge of the sea, my friend and I floated as the twins swam around us, splashing us when we looked away.

"I want to swim with you," red floaties said to me. "Will you take out my ponytail holder?"

I fixed her hair the way I would my own niece's. Thin-faced twin pushed her sister aside in the sea. "I have a ponytail, too. Fix it?"

This, in short, is my life in Miami.

I am a Midwestern Pinay, raised in Milwaukee and transplanted to Miami like some hybrid apple-mango-bamboo stalk of wheat. Prior to the late 1950s, when it was still culturally the Deep South, locals called it Miam-ah. But then Cubans, fleeing Castro, began coming here in one wave after another. Others followed, immigrating here from nations like Chile, Columbia, and Ecuador. The city began to look more like the capital of Latin America than a Southern city. As Miami grew internationally, I was coming of age in Wisconsin.

My childhood consisted of hot cereals and layers of sweaters, rubber boots and crocheted scarves. My body knew the crunch of snow underfoot, the breath that turned icy through woolen masks, and the chill of dark winter mornings.

Growing up, my family was the only Filipino family in the neighborhood. My brothers were called "Chinks" and "Japs" and got into fist fights. Parents accused them of using black belt Karate on their classmates. But for a girl of color growing up in Midwestern-nice Wisconsin, micro-aggressions were subtle. I made the pom-pom squad, for example, but I was never invited to slumber parties. No boy in my school ever asked me out (not that my parents would have allowed me to go). I had normalized these experiences because it was all I knew.

I recently saw a black and white photo of me and my pom-pom squad in high school. We were dressed in wool mini-skirts and boxy sweaters with giant B's on our chests. We stood shoulder to shoulder. All in uniform. I was among the taller girls in the back, the last one in the upper left corner. Between me and the girl next to me, Jackie, was a space wide enough for another girl. I had never noticed that space until now. Out of twenty-four pom-pom girls, three of us were girls of color. One Latina, one Japanese American, and me.

And then I moved to Miami in 2002.

The doors at MIA swung open and the humidity washed over me amid the beep-beep of taxis and the cacophony of so many languages. Suddenly, I was home. This was not only Miami, this was Manila too. From the traffic on US 1, to the resort blue waters of the Atlantic, there was symmetry between these two cities. During my Fulbright in Manila, I regularly sat in traffic for two hours to move twelve miles. I was used to this. From the international quality of the people, to the little markets on Calle Ocho and the way friends and neighbors greeted each other with besitos on the cheek, Miami felt like home.

My parents visited and said, "Miami is like Manila before Marcos." They meant the Spanish style houses, the Latin surnames, the brown faces we saw during mass. They were talking about Filipinos we ran into in restaurants.

My father and mother met in the mid-1950s in Milwaukee. He was a medical resident from Macabebe, Pampanga, and she was a graduate student of English literature from Quezon City, Metro Manila. Before settling in Wisconsin, our family lived in seven cities. I was born in Harrisburg, Pennsylvania. We moved to Baltimore, Maryland, and Wilson, North Carolina, before heading back to Manila for two years. I was a toddler, just learning to speak, when we left Manila. The vestigial memories I have of living in Manila are what make Miami home.

Is it possible that my ancestors are calling to me from seven thousand islands? That when I hear the waves on the shores of South Beach, I am listening to the tide in Pitogo? And when I stroll Bayfront Park, am I actually walking Luneta Park? I ask because my body remembers this heat, the humidity, these waters. I am at ease sitting in a sea of traffic, meditating in a garden of palm trees and whistling bamboo. Rice, beans, plantains, and fried eggs are comfort food. My body says this is home.

We are a city of outsiders—we come from every nation. I have lived in many cities and many rural towns. I have been an outsider almost all my life, but in Miami we are all displaced. We are all half-dreaming of going home—Camaguey, Port au Prince, Buenos Aires, Milwaukee, and Manila. All the outsiders live inside Miami.

The familiarity of what I cannot know from experience soothes me. At first, I went to the beach almost every weekend. My skin color deepened. People mistook me for Chinese Jamaican. I walked into grocery stores where clerks spoke to me in Spanish. And I would say, "¡No me digas!" like a local. We'd laugh. "¡Qué cómico!" People treated me like one of them.

I can hold a conversation in Spanish, but when it gets malalim—deep—I mix my languages. When I am confused, instead of "¿Cómo?," I ask, "Ano?" The intonation is the same in both languages.

When I returned from my Fulbright, the cab driver spoke to me in Spanish. "¿De dónde eres?" he wanted to know. I was slow to respond. In Manila, I had spent the last year speaking Tagalog.

"Ako'y Amerikana," I replied.

"Soy de Honduras," he answered, unfazed.

In 2009, years before I married, I moved to a neighborhood along Coral Way, a historic urban boulevard that runs through Miami and into Coral Gables. My house had been built in 1939 along with other bungalows and Mission Revival style homes. Everyone on my street spoke Spanish.

My casita stood between two houses of the same style, and within these houses lived viejas. On the right, there were three widowed sisters—Marta, Olga, and Paula. On the left was Elsa, also a viuda. The women were best friends, and I'd see them on the sidewalk in front of my house, sometimes laughing, sometimes shouting in anger. Right away, they befriended me. They called me "China" even though I told them, "Yo soy Evelina, la filipina. No soy China." They laughed, calling me "China" anyway.

Elsa was small and quiet. From afar, I never knew how she was feeling, but face to face, I could see it in her eyes and in the path of her delicate wrinkles. Every day I noticed her standing by the chain-link fence in her front yard, watching the street, waiting for the mail, and talking to passersby.

One afternoon I brought her a mango from my tree.

At her kitchen table, Elsa recounted the story of her life. She had suffered bouts of depression since she came to this country. Never in Cuba, only in this country. She wouldn't even say it—the United States of America. Solamente en este país, pero nunca en Cuba. These days, she told me, she felt nervous constantly. Everyone she loved had died—su mamá y papá, su esposo y hermana. Seven years ago, her husband and sister had died months apart. Though she had the abuela sisters, who took her everywhere, and a daughter in Boston, she couldn't calm her nerves. The noise of her memories crowded her head, kept her up at night.

We sat for a long time. She picked up the mango, smelled it, and handed it to me. "Qué rico," she said.

I told her she needed a novio. She laughed.

It is hard for me to imagine Miam-ah when it was part of the Deep South. My dad often told us stories of his days in Wilson, North Carolina. We moved there right after I was born in 1961. At the hospital, the guard asked him to walk through the "Whites Only" doors in the front. My dad pointed to his skin, "But look! I am not white." His patients went in through the "Colored" door in the back. "My patients are right here," he reasoned.

"Sorry, Doc," the guard said. "If you want to see them, you're going to have to go around."

But when my father filled up the car at gas stations, attendants directed him to the "Colored" bathrooms.

We were neither black nor white.

What would my father's experience have been in Miam-ah? Similar?

My connection to this city is instinctual. It is the air, the bamboo, the salt water. But it is also cultural. Like Cuba, the Philippines—also an island culture—was colonized by the Spanish and "liberated" by the United States. We share the same oppressors. Similar food. And even certain words. If Miami were Miam-ah today, with its ocean waves and tropical foliage, would I still belong? Would my body connect to this metro island culture?

These days, my garden with its avocado, mango, lemon, and naranja agria trees brings me back to my grandmother's in Manila—especially to the stillness I find there every morning. I have my little statue of Mama Mary, and in the shade of the day, when I close my eyes, listening to the clicking bamboo stalks and the distant traffic of Coral Way, I am transported in time and space. I am home. ◉

Treacherous Joy:
An Epistle to the South

Tiana Clark

> *The ache for home lives in all of us.*
> —Dr. Maya Angelou

DEAR TENNESSEE, I THOUGHT I HATED YOU—
I didn't love you until I left you.

I wasn't born in the South, which was the initial problem. I was born in Los Angeles near the lip of the Pacific Ocean. I said California was my home even after I moved to Nashville at seven. I wanted to be from somewhere else. I loved being from the West Coast and I said it for years and years after I moved. I said it for so long, even when it didn't make sense, because I had lived in Nashville longer. My friends made fun of me, but I didn't care. I didn't want to lose the soundtrack of waves in my ears. The seashells I kept in my pocket.

I remember hearing "y'all" and thinking it sounded like a twang of something familiar, a musical note I couldn't pinpoint. It was slow and viscous—not like honey or molasses, but more like fresh mud—and I wanted to repeat it under my breath each time I heard it, but my mother wouldn't let me. I wasn't allowed to say "ain't" or "ma'am" either, each contraction possessing a Southern, syrupy sway.

Tennessee, your geography was strange and claustrophobic to me in 1991—the trees like broccoli tops bunched every hill—hills everywhere, close like fertile breasts jutting from the earth in patterns that seemed particular to this region; bumpy braille from the terrain, so many golden whorls of pollen clouds, divots and dots, lines of greenery, and so many trees— trees for miles. I didn't know their names. Still don't, besides the magnolia. I know that tree for its wide, waxy leaves and creamy blooms. To love a landscape felt elusive and abstract to me as a kid. Still does. What does it mean to be tethered to the psyche of a state? California smeared into dream logic, vague and faraway, hard to remember each day, just bluish watercolors blossoming at the rim of my early memories—dissolving—except for the lone cactus in our backyard. I remember our neighbors asked for the nopales when the spines started poking through the jade-colored pads.

The South seemed lush and stuffed with churches, but hostile and impenetrable, too. Do you remember the first time I was called a nigger? I was roller-skating at my church's daycare. There were two white, Southern boys on roller skates, spinning around my small circumference, calling me this new, burning word. I didn't know what the word meant, but my body blackened wrong with heat, and I knew this little song was only meant for me. I felt those two-barbed g's stinging my eight-year-old skin—and poof—just like that, I knew I was different. The change was immediate and my mouth tasted like fresh blood and pennies. I wasn't bleeding, but something akin to despair loosened and leaked inside me, made me feel dizzy.

The word was personal and singular in its spectacular aim. The shrapnel of that speech shattered something slightly unspeakable in me, something I still can't fully articulate. My skin started to itch and sweat. This wild word made me want to weep but I didn't. This wild word made me want to hate myself. I think this might have been the first time I wanted to die or felt like dying or maybe I just wanted to disappear. How do you become unseen once you've been seen so clearly? I was standing in the middle of their spinning, caught in their invisible web, static. I remember wishing my skin had a zipper, so that I could shed myself from the mud. This two-syllable word had heft and history, because it felt heavier each time the two boys punched the epithet at my face, penetrating the dark juice in my delicate bones. They kept laughing and pointing, their pinched, white faces repeating *nigger,*

nigger, nigger like a little song, taunting. I can still hear them singing if I want to hurt myself again.

I had this early inkling that I wanted to escape, to run away and live in fantastical New York or move back to Los Angeles. In my prepubescent mind, things would be better somewhere else, somewhere outside the geometric shape of your state, a parallelogram tilting east, a four-sided figure. I thought the shape of another state was what was missing in me.

I wanted to escape the South and the two nooses left on our back porch (one for mom and one for me). My mom didn't tell me about the nooses till I was much older. She didn't want to terrify me as a child. Years later she said they were hung up in sloppy knots after the first night we moved into our one bedroom apartment in Brentwood, Tennessee, a welcome gift from our new white neighbors. Sometimes I still imagine her there on our small back porch—alone, a single, Black mother—looking at those crude death symbols swaying, imagining my little neck and then hers, breaking, thinking everything she had ever thought about the South coming true before her like two pendulous omens exploding. She called her friends who took them down and prayed for our protection. My mother never touched the ropes.

Tennessee, I wanted to leave and escape the origins of the KKK in Pulaski and the eighty oxidized Confederate monuments, some weathered by the tint of pea-green patina. I wanted to escape the Jacuzzi-steam of summer heat and plantation weddings. I wanted to leave the rapid-paced gentrification of East and North Nashville and Wedgewood Houston or, rather, WeHo. Nashville was becoming the *new* Nashville, which meant it was whiter and richer with more cranes slicing the ever-changing skyline; streets I'd known for years became less recognizable to me. The constant development was annoying, but after the 2016 election, I was actively looking for a way out of the South, away from the river of blood-red counties engulfing Davidson County, the lone blue dot. Racists weren't afraid anymore. They had a megaphone in the White House, and I didn't know how to carry myself in public (or in private really).

The Midwest was my volta, my turn to veer from the South. I leapt at the chance to move to Madison, Wisconsin in the summer of 2017 for a poetry fellowship. I was ready for squeaky cheese curds and cold winters. I wanted to follow what seemed like the concrete drinking gourd up north. I wanted to be carried away toward freedom in my U-Haul, which sounded like a massive garbage disposal on wheels, droning on I-57 through Effingham and Champion, then Bloomington and Rockford. The night breeze was perfect when we finally arrived; just warm enough with no thickness to it, thin as water, and just as refreshing, too. I remember thinking this was a good sign. But in the morning, I didn't trust all the Black Lives Matter signs stippled across the manicured lawns of my white neighborhood. In the sunshine, the town seemed to have a self-satisfied sheen to it.

During my year living in Wisconsin, an employee at a fancy grocery store followed me around as if I was stealing. I was ogled at restaurants. I often had to change seats with my spouse so I wouldn't have to watch old, white people watching me, gawking. Their glare wasn't out of disgust, but rather fish-out-of-water googly eyes, and I was the big, Black fish at a bougie restaurant staring back, unashamed but annoyed. I hardly saw or interacted with any Black people outside of the university. I was lonely, but this was a different brand of isolation that blossomed, bloated, and made walking the edge of the isthmus hazy and apocalyptic, especially when the lakes froze over and the horizon was creamy and you couldn't tell where the hard water ended and the vague milk-filled sky began. The racism in Madison was opaque, more psychological. I didn't see any Confederate flags, but I felt more uncomfortable in my hyper-visible body as if I was twenty feet tall. I was never called the n-word while I lived there, but why was I starting to feel like one?

Oh, Tennessee—I began to miss you. I was starting to look back at the South, longing like Lot's wife, except this time I didn't transform into a monument made of salt. I didn't want to be punished for my regret or curiosity. Nashville was suddenly home, and I scared myself with how much I wanted to go back.

"Racism Is Everywhere, So Why Not Move South?" is the title of Reniqua Allen's brilliant op-ed from the New York Times, which traces this recent migratory trend back South for Black Millennials. Allen speaks with Jessica M. Barron, a demographer and sociologist out of Durham, North Carolina, who says, "There is something about black millennials wanting to find some type of reclaiming or resurgence in terms of moving back to the South, reclaiming the South as a place where black folks can thrive."

There is no promised land—anywhere. No heaven for Black folks hovering above the Mason-Dixon line. If I am not safe anywhere, then why don't I just come back home? Why not keep fighting where I flourish? At least I can be close to my mom in Chattanooga and restaurants that serve real sweet tea split by fresh lemons and sweet potato pie that makes you stomp your feet, as well as the original hot chicken recipe from Prince's that stains the soppy, white bread underneath with hallelujah heat. Dear Tennessee, racism sure does make you hungry and I haven't been well fed since I left two years ago.

I want Jacob Lawrence to paint a reverse Migration Series, but he is dead now and his paintings are divided by the odd and even numbers between two museums. Instead, I imagine the new paintings: the repetition of Black folks flattened and abstracted by casein tempera and gesso on wood panels, this time coming back down South on airplanes and cars, phones in our

hands, crowning headphones and vibrant colors—
hot pinks and lime greens instead of warm, earthy
tones. We are a murmuring of glossy black starlings
coming back home now. The Southern cities at the
top of the first panel would read: Atlanta, Miami,
and New Orleans. It would continue with narratives
detailing a thriving Black middle class with snatched,
slick edges, box braids and Afro puffs. Black execu-
tives and Black-owned businesses like Slim & Husky's
Pizza, started by three Tennessee State University
graduates in North Nashville, or Cupcake Collection
in Germantown, opened by a family transplanted by
Hurricane Katrina.

I'm ready to come back home—not necessarily
to a real house or a home state—but back to wres-
tle with that fountainhead idea from James Baldwin,
that "home is not a place but simply an irrevocable
condition," a final state of being, an irreparable safety
that I carry within my own consciousness. I harbor a
treacherous joy no matter where I reside. This is why
I keep returning obsessively to the happy disobedience
of Icarus and my indifference to him failing and falling. Meaning, we've gotten the story all wrong. We've
focused on the end of the myth. Maybe the lesson was
that he escaped. I forgot about the joy and giddiness
of freedom and what that does to a newly freed body
in flight.

It's true—the sweltering sun in the South feels
hotter than anywhere else in July. I thought home

wasn't supposed to hurt, but everywhere hurts to live, so I want to come back home to the hurt I know best. The hurt I know how to circumspect and map, trace the contours of its face with my two index fingers. I'm coming back to driving up and down the long guitar neck of I-65, ordering hash brown casserole at Cracker Barrel, where I worked one summer when I was fifteen with a name tag that said Jesús, but people still called me Jesus.

I don't have a sense of the resolution just yet, but I feel this ember for Nashville flickering a red glow inside me. I think of *Cane* by Jean Toomer, on returning: "If I could feel that I came to the South to face it. If I, the dream (not what is weak and afraid in me) could become the face of the South. How my lips would sing for it, my songs being the lips of its soul. Soul. Soul hell." Tennessee—I just like the way my blackness, my Black ache and bliss, my Black imagination, my Black way of being in the South sifts through you like a gospel choir when the Holy Ghost thunderclaps on Sunday mornings, but I'm listening from outside the building, the reckoning just out of reach. I can't make out every word, just the swell of divine, Black voices rapt—which is to say that is the best way I can describe my tenderness for you. ⊙

Nuisance: An Essay about Home

Latria Graham

THE WATER COMES WHILE I AM ASLEEP AND IT IS only when I hear my dog barking her high-pitched *something is different and I need your attention right now* bark that I realize we are in trouble.

Ice-cold terror hits the pit of my stomach and runs out towards my wrists, making it hard to use my hands, even though I know I only have a few minutes to get moving.

This whole thing is my fault, I tell myself. I forgot to check the drains around my house before going to bed. Dealing with the drains used to be my daddy's job, but he died a couple of years ago. My mother had back surgery so she can't do it, and my little brother lives three-thousand miles away, so I am the keeper of the grounds when I am home.

This year, spring came in early March (it comes earlier every year) and the pollen strings from the giant oak tree in my yard cover everything—cars, trees, even animals if they stay still long enough. The wind blows the strings to the ground and they accumulate in the corners of our property, where the drains for our street happen to be. The drains were never meant to receive this much rainfall and the detritus slows down the water's ability to exit our backyard. The hurricane-magnitude downpour that arrives in the middle of the night overwhelms the 1970s engineering of the house. When there is nowhere for the water to go, it invites itself inside.

By the time I tug on my anorak and boots, the bottom floor of my house will be standing in almost a foot of water, mini waves licking the first two steps in the foyer, wondering if it could find a way to reach the second floor.

Part human negligence, part natural catastrophe, my insurance man has a name for what is happening: nuisance flooding. His tone on the other end of the phone when I call him and tell him what has happened implies that I'm the nuisance, that I should have known better, that I am not a good homeowner. He hangs up and I make my way back outside, standing in knee-high water in the pouring rain, pulling pollen strings from the drain cover with my bare hands.

Nuisance flooding—not big enough to warrant structural concern. Not big enough to be a catastrophe to anybody but us.

My daddy's side is a farming family that is five generations deep, so we see every roadblock as a new thing to get over, but not the thing that could stop us. I wonder what my ancestors would say about the weather now, about all the things I can count that are changing in my world: the way our crops perform, the abundance of hot, sticky nights that didn't use to exist, the lack of lightning bugs at night.

Twenty years ago, my grandma sent out warnings, trying to tell folks that things were changing. She was deemed a nuisance. I think back to what the man from State Farm said. This is my home, this is my community, and I can't just give up on it. I can't let what I have float away, even if the insurance man will never understand.

Life happens on the top floor—that's where all of our bedrooms are, and the kitchen. The things on the ground floor, the stuff I'm feverishly hoisting to higher ground, is what makes life worth living—my dead daddy's vinyl record collection, my brother's art, the thousands of books I have piled up to the ceiling, each bookcase from a different chapter of my life. My mama's ambitions live down there, tethered to her sewing machine, her room of dreams, the only thing that remains of her time spent at the Fashion Institute of Technology in NYC, where she trained to be a fashion designer. When she graduated, her parents pressured her to come back home, where she married my dad, who sought to leave his farming roots far behind. They bumbled their way towards what they thought happily ever after was supposed to look like. They had children, created careers, and eventually bought this house. For my brother and me, this house was a beacon—no matter where we've traveled for work, we have always been able to come back home. If we were coming in late, mom and dad would leave the light on.

I have had the same house key my entire life and I am so used to the *slip* and *click* sound when I turn the knob that I have a Pavlovian response. As soon as the door opens, my shoulders slump and my muscles relax. I am home.

I wonder how long I'll get to feel that way. Things are starting to change. Dad is gone. The water continues to rise.

Between 1997, when my parents purchased this house, and 2017, it has flooded four times in total. In the last 365 days, the house has flooded three times. We modify, we adjust. We always have. We put everything we care for in plastic bins to keep the damp out. I try to check the drains weekly, but as a traveling journalist I am on the road 120 days of the year, and that routine sometimes falls to the wayside.

Carelessness always creeps in and we start leaving our things around the way people living in houses do—a favorite book is left on a low-lying table in the den, piles of sewing patterns mama was sorting through the night before stacked neatly on the floor. By the time I make it downstairs, these items will be ruined, victims of the rapidly churning cold water that is steadily creeping towards my knees. Each time the rains come we lose a little more of ourselves. I wonder how much black history we've lost—first edition books, records from my father's time at an HBCU, my mama's recollections of the Obamas entering the White House. Black history is so fragile, that I see anything tangible as valuable, and I am crushed when I think of all that has been lost to disaster—floods, fires, and terror.

Arms tired and tingling, back hurting from the excess weight I've put on this year due to overwork and stress, my body wants to leave what I own to the water, but my heart won't let me. This house, this little acre on a map with my mama's name on it, may be the only proof that my family has made it, that the mason's daughter and the farmer's son could come together and buy a two-story stand-alone home in a large subdivision on Spartanburg's Westside, proof of middle-class Black American existence. For me this house isn't a status symbol, but rather a reminder of what's possible now: this address gives me some stability—because this place exists, I can be a full-time writer.

This address also gives me the ability to vote, and I exercise that right every chance I get. The land around here is imbued with voting rights history that I refuse to just let die. Five miles away from here, when emancipated slaves went to go vote for the first time, they were terrorized. Some were whipped. Others watched as the ears were cut off of their loved ones. Hooded men burned down their houses.

Later, in the 1940s, up near the northern part of the county line, an African American woman named Lottie Polk Gaffney tried to exercise her right to vote. She too lost everything.

I know I can vote from anywhere, but something about voting here feels too important to lose.

Cast off pages of my first draft of a story float past me, the pages clumping together, my editing marks now illegible smeared ink. Last night, before all of this, I was writing about Princeville, North Carolina. Founded by emancipated slaves, it is the oldest incorporated African American town in the country, and it has been wiped off of the map twice by floods.

After Hurricane Matthew ripped through the town in 2016, the residents were given three options: rebuild everything all over again, hoping the new structures could stand the floods (it is a given that there would be more floods), pick up the entire town and move it all farther from the river, or accept a buyout from the federal government and move somewhere else, abandoning Princeville altogether. For two years I've gone back and forth to this little town, sitting in on city council meetings, wondering what the end was gonna be, what the residents would choose. If the dam near the town was raised any higher, it would flood the mostly white established town of Tarboro. So the government keeps building the dam back the same way, with small modifications. The officials over infrastructure won't return my calls about the dam, and I'm pretty sure after ten voicemails, left weekly, I am deemed a nuisance—the nosy reporter who wants to know what will happen to history, who can't let things just be, who doesn't realize that the North Carolina establishment likes the old way just fine. My draft doesn't have an ending, so before bed I tossed the sheets to the side for recycling. I didn't expect it to be carried back to me the next day on the water.

I have made my career by crafting stories that highlight the resilience of people living in tense places: a football game after police protests in Charlotte, North Carolina, large powwows near Standing Rock, North Dakota, a roller derby bout at a rink in Flint, Michigan. I collect these stories and figure out what they have to say about our country, and all of the ways in which we are failing our citizens. I write them because I want readers to see all of the ways we can be better, to see opportunities to help one another.

I haven't turned in the Princeville story because I haven't figured out how to sum up what Princeville's trials say about America. I wonder what this Gordian knot says about me. I can't save my own house. What makes me believe I can save a whole town?

I don't have the money to fix my drain problem. Contractors say they believe French drains may save our overtaxed established ones, but it is a five-thousand-dollar science experiment. My mind tells me if I had that much money to spare, it might be better to just clean up the place and put the damn thing on the market. In the end this is how we'll be moved—barely surviving disaster after disaster, until they break our resilience, until we can no longer adapt, and this house and my soul are just a shell. I realize I'm battling so much more than just water—the ever-encroaching threat of poverty, my mother's illness, my own depression and sense of fatalism. I want something better for Princeville. I hope they get it. I want to write a better ending.

Eventually it stops raining. I'll lose a day's pay sifting through the remnants of our things, seeing what I can save. We will go back to being careful for as long as we can remember to be, even though our old habits will return eventually. I think carefully, analytically, about how I can keep this from happening again. I turn on the television and see other people battling this type of low-stakes flooding. At the moment, I am an indicator of other people's suffering. That, I think, I can do something about.

I start making phone calls to local officials. "Hi— my name is Latria Graham, and I live in Spartanburg County. Let's just say that I'll be your new nuisance." ◉

Are You Muslim? and Other Questions White Landlords Ask Me

Aruni Kashyap

I AM ON MY WAY TO LOOK FOR A NEW LIVING SPACE that I need starting this summer. It has been hard looking for a place. The leasing cycle in this city works like the semester system. Just like how you can't enroll in a course in the middle of the semester, it is next to impossible to find an apartment in a preferred location during what they call the "off season."

I have been living in Athens, Georgia, for one and a half years, but this is the first time I am looking for a house on my own. When I first moved here, it was December and everyone was busy enjoying the holidays. The streets were deserted and the town felt lonely. A generous colleague drove me around the deserted city, looking for apartments. He was a tall man in a black jacket. It was hard not to like him because he addressed everyone as *ma'am* and *sir*, because he always smiled while talking, and because he listened to people with the patience of a therapist. Feeling reassured, and slightly jet-lagged, I let him handle most of the conversations with leasing agents, landlords, and receptionists at rental agencies.

I was grateful that it wasn't too cold in Georgia. When the leasing officer said that she couldn't rent it to me because I didn't have a credit history in the country, it was my colleague who stepped ahead to speak on my behalf, presenting a request she couldn't walk away from, "Ma'am, if you don't mind, can we please explain the situation to you?" First, he thanked her for being patient with us, thanked her for running my credit history, and then explained to her the funny problem of not having a credit history because I had just immigrated to this country a week ago.

"He is going to have a credit history, and you wouldn't have any problem with him as your tenant." He looked at me and suggested, "Maybe you could show them your contract with the university?"

Last week, I made thirty phone calls and viewed seven possible places to rent. Since it is the off season, my options are limited. When a colleague tells me about a home that would suit my needs (two bedrooms, around twelve-hundred dollars, not far from downtown Athens), I look it up immediately.

The house is a little over my budget, but I have told myself that if I love something, I will take it. If I can imagine myself doing housework in my underwear, I would rent it.

The house has a sunroom, two bedrooms, and two bathrooms.

I love the sunroom. I would like to sit and read with a cup of hardboiled cardamom tea, and my henna hair-mask and sandalwood face pack on. There is a clean backyard with a dead tree and a storage room. My mother would have disapproved of this dead tree: *You need things that are alive and growing around you, not a tall dead tree.*

But there is something beautiful about this tree with its branches outstretched to the skies as if begging for rains. The local bookshop, my favorite one, is in the vicinity. I attend many events there. Good cafes that sell turmeric tea are less than a mile away. There is also an excellent vegan restaurant, though I am a proud omnivore. And just to be clear, I don't drink turmeric tea. What I mean is that this is the "cool part of town"—most of my colleagues and students think so. I am often told, this is the liberal part of Athens. When I drive through the neighborhood, I see so many blue-colored STACEY ABRAMS FOR GOVERNOR signs in front of pretty little houses.

The yard is lined with shrubs and plants. The

neighborhood is quiet. I take out my phone and note down things: rent, power, gas, square feet, rental insurance, maintenance. I like what I am seeing, and as we move from room to room, I fall in love with the house.

"Maybe you can sit down on a Sunday with a book here," the lady says, standing in the sunroom. In reply, I smile and nod my head. I like that she suggests the idea of reading a book.

The husband, who is wearing a white polo shirt, assures me that I can call him to take care of anything, "Any maintenance issue," he says, "you can call me anytime."

The rooms aren't massive, but they aren't small. I imagine placing my queen bed in the bedroom. I am sure I would be able to fit in a dresser and a couple of bookcases. I have a lot of books. I keep books even in my bedroom, on my bed's headstand, on the bedside table. I am always buying bookshelves.

"You asked about natural light." The woman steps into one of the bedrooms and pulls the blinds. "You will get ample natural light. The second bedroom receives the afternoon's light, you know?"

I like the couple most when they tell me that they attend events at my favorite bookshop and when they name professors who work at my university, asking me if I know them. I tell them that my university is huge and there are thousands of professors. They nod in agreement. They say that the university is huge, and that you could work there for decades without knowing most people. I nod back. We have a bond.

I decide to rent the house. I tell them that I love what I have seen, but hold off on telling them about my decision because I have another home to view that day.

The husband and wife look like people who would vote for Stacey Abrams. I like them. They are chatty and warm, and they bitch about rental companies that prey on young students who "come to our country for education, and we treat them like shit by exploiting them."

But it is a small question from the lady that ticks me off.

"So, I was just wondering, you know—I mean— are you a Muslim?"

Later, a friend of mine would tell me that it is illegal to ask questions about my religion. Another friend would be furious to hear this, but I laugh about it.

When the couple asks me if I am a Muslim, I am just exhausted. Perhaps, I don't want to accept that these people, who are funny and chatty and sensitive about immigrant students, who are astonished that I am a professor—*Oh wow, you must be so intelligent that they hired you from India*—are just like everybody else.

I have heard variations of their question from

landlords, colleagues from other departments, and cab drivers.

I am actually born a Hindu though I don't care much about my religion. I am not an atheist. I eat beef. I have Saraswati statues in my house because Saraswati is the Goddess of Learning, like Minerva, but I never pray to her. I have her statues because she is a stunning goddess who refused to marry, and she traveled on the back of a giant white swan with a black bindi on her forehead and a red lotus in one of her hands.

Is this the answer the couple was looking for?

Are you a Muslim?

I look around for a chair to sit, but we are outside the house now, in the front yard. I am about to leave. It is almost noon, and there is a lot more to do, such as view another house, buy groceries, and search websites for apartments, but I feel like taking a nap. I just want to go home and lie in my bed and stare at the white ceiling.

I say, "Excuse me?"

I think about the several places I have viewed—good areas where good white people live with other non-white people from around the world, people who would probably vote for Stacey Abrams again. I think about the apartment on Dearing Street that I found on Facebook. After viewing the apartment rented by a young lady, we talked about the huge sectional that she had bought from a store called Anthropologie. She said she had only received two queries, including one from me. She was in a hurry to get out of her lease. The other query was from a "young freshman" who couldn't move in until August.

I said, "Then it is a great fit for me." I said that I would confirm after an hour, once I viewed the apartment on Prince Avenue, another "cool" part of the town. When I texted her later that day, I thought about the adequate natural light the house received and where I would place my writing desk. I was sure my house hunting was over. To my surprise, I received a text: *Sorry, the other girl applied and got approved.*

Last week, I also looked at a townhome on South Milledge Avenue, next to my favorite Chinese restaurant. The townhome was available in the summer, was just the size I needed it to be, and the right price. I told the manager that I liked the townhome and would rent it. He promised to email me a lease. I stopped looking for houses, relieved that my house hunting was finally over.

When the lease didn't reach me, I gave him a few days, and then sent a message. I emailed him after six days, left a voicemail after ten, called and texted again after two weeks—no response. I had started to feel like a stalker. In the meantime, the other houses I could have rented were snatched away.

Last week, I also visited an apartment in a filthy neighborhood where the grass was tall and bugs fine like pollen entered my nose, making me sneeze as I walked toward the door. Inside, a young man, perhaps in his late twenties, greeted me. The apartment smelled. A beagle growled at me from a cage, and a gun was on the dining table as if it were home decor.

I don't want to look for apartments anymore, and that's why I feel like resting on a bed for several hours. That's why I say, "Excuse me?"

Actually, I know what to tell them to get this house. I could say to them, *No, I am not a Muslim*, and they would laugh, and I would laugh awkwardly, and I would get the house. After all, unlike the landlord of the house on Carlton Street, as if to test my knowledge when they hear what I do for a living, they haven't asked me "Who is your favorite American author?"

At least, like the landlord of the two-bedroom apartment on Boulevard, they aren't asking, "Can you also teach Shakespeare? Do you know where 'To be or not to be' is from? Hahaha!"

They haven't asked me with lifted brows, like that landlord who told me about his guru in Delhi and asked, "You teach the English language?"

And when I answered, "No, I teach English literature," he asked me again, "I mean, do you also teach American kids?"

"Yes," I replied after a pause.

He showed me two horrible houses.

One landlord went on to quiz me further about my responsibilities: Was I a professor who also taught graduate students or "just undergrads who need ESL help?"

This constant questioning is so wearing.

I can say that I am a Hindu and solve this problem. But I do not. I could use my Hindu privilege to get this house because it is so tempting, because I am exhausted, but I am not sure if I would be able to sleep well in this house if I do.

I want to say, *I am sorry, ma'am, how is that question relevant? I am a writer and teacher, that's all that matters.*

Instead, I say, "I am not comfortable answering the question." I am not sure why I am so polite.

After a pause, the husband laughs loudly. Too loudly, in fact. Too cheerfully. It is the kind of awkward laughter that acknowledges guilt but tries to laugh it away. "Oh, that doesn't matter," he says.

Flustered, the lady tells me, "But you asked so much about the sun—if this house will get enough natural light? So we thought…"

I want to ask them back: *Don't white people like natural light in their houses?*

But I don't.

I smile.

I laugh at their jokes.

I exit politely, promising to get back to them, though, of course, I won't. ◉

Auntie

Minda Honey

IN 2008, I MOVED TO ORANGE COUNTY, CALIFOR-
nia. I was twenty-three years old. I smelled the salt of
the ocean, I drank juice squeezed from oranges I picked
with my own hands, and I believed that I would never
ever move back home. I would not miss the mosquitos, the humidity, or the blank gaze of confederate
monuments. I decided I would not miss Louisville,
Kentucky, at all.

I grew up in a neither-here-nor-there place just
as likely to be described as the Midwest as it is the
South. But I call myself Southern because my mouth
knows the language of sweet tea in the summertime

and black-eyed peas on New Year's Day. Because the sounds of letters tumble backward into the curve of my tongue when I speak. Because the Mason-Dixon Line lays fat along the upper-border of Kentucky.

Eight years after I moved out West, my middle sister had a baby and I moved back home.

I was then thirty-one and, although I was the oldest of us three sisters, the idea of being a parent was still foreign to me. Nearly none of my California friends had children. My sister, who is three years younger than me, had been in a relationship with her husband for several years and their dreams included, but were not limited to, good careers and a house and a family. My dreams were different. I wanted my IUD to continue to function properly as promised by the medical community. I wanted to be with a man whose feelings weren't a series of unsolved mysteries. And I wanted to write a book.

It was my graduation from an MFA program that prompted me to box up my possessions, then send them off in a FedEx Ground shipment and drive my car cross-country. The low cost of living in Louisville would mean I could focus full-time on becoming a "professional" writer. My soon-to-be niece was an afterthought.

I arrived a week after Elliot was born. The first time I held Ellie, I supported her in my palms like a server at a seafood restaurant presenting the catch of the day. I could count on one hand the number of times I'd held a baby. I'd never been left alone with one and had never changed a diaper. I had no intimate knowledge of the panic a baby's cry can summon or how all thoughts are overtaken by baby even when baby is sleeping peacefully nearby. The concern never ceased. This was what it was like to be parent-adjacent. This was what it was like to be an auntie.

My mom—her sisters back in the Philippines—raised us to call her Filipina friends "Auntie." My mom was the first among her friends to learn to drive. They'd pile more of us kids than was legal into the backseat, and if we were lucky, head to the park, but usually we ended up at the mall. These women smoked the same Capri 120s my mom smoked, had the same white rice cooker with the watercolor flowers on its belly she had, and when we got out of line, clucked at us in the same language we didn't understand. They were like my mother in infinite replication.

My dad has six sisters. It was Auntie Jay we spent the most time with. My parents divorced when I was twelve and it was Auntie Jay who gave me a copy of *Their Eyes Were Watching God* thinking it was actually about God and that religion would help me overcome the heartache of my family come undone. I'm thankful for how wrong she was about that book and for bringing Zora Neale Hurston's Janie into my life. Janie with her eyes ever to the sky, Janie who knew something about being Black and woman and Southern and lusting after self-possession.

Auntie Jay dragged us to her Southern Baptist church on all the major religious holidays. She hauled us down the pews to pray in the New Year until the year I turned sixteen and could drive away from her. When I was real little she wrote us letters from a cruise she'd gone on. My mother would read them aloud to us. It wasn't until I was grown that I understood she'd actually gone to rehab. And by the time I'd moved back to Louisville, she was once again adrift on the same dark sea that had swept her away from family all those many years ago to that place where loved ones are spoken of in past tense even before they've passed.

Auntie Jay was my mother's favorite of my father's sisters. She'd wrap my mom's homegrown long hair around her fist, give a small yank and teasingly ask, "What horse did you get this from?" Auntie Jay with her nails always done. Auntie Jay with her gold jewelry always shining. Auntie Jay with the best cheesecakes and the husband who fried the best fish. My mom and Auntie Jay would sit at the kitchen table or out on Auntie Jay's concrete slab front porch in lawn chairs woven from alternating wide ribbons of nylon, cigarettes lit, gossip slipping from their lips all night long.

I don't remember as a child ever looking at those two women in deep communion with one another and wondering what I would be like as a mother or an aunt or what silent lessons little girls would learn from me about being a woman. But what becomes of the memories a watermelon seed holds of the flesh of the fruit? Everything. The seed grows to be that which it came from.

A little more than a year after my move home, I rented half of a blue duplex two blocks from my sister and her husband and my niece. When Ellie began to piece together crumbs of words, she did not call me auntie, she called me Min-Min, doubling up the first half of my name.

I feed her. I bathe her. I am on the emergency call list at the daycare. Every summer for one week, I care for her while her parents take a trip by themselves. I have traveled with them as a family.

I have watched my niece, her little legs losing the shake of uncertainty with every day she grows older, run toward me in the airport, and have asked myself, *How can a love as vast as the Milky Way fit in space the size of my heart?*

There is one night in Louisville, where it's still warm enough to be outside without a jacket and the humidity has fallen away, the mosquitos less of a nuisance, that my sister and Ellie come over to my house. We sit on my steps and our baby sister joins us. There's Ellie in the center protected by the trifecta; her caramel half-waves, half-curls hair always in motion as if caught on a breeze that blows only for her, sitting up tall because she wants to see it all, be part of it all. Yes, there's Ellie, there's us. Just us, no skinny cigarettes and no nylon lawn chairs, but the gossip slips just as easy from our lips as our love for her slips from our hearts. ◉

Outta the Souf

Regina Bradley

I WOULDN'T APPRECIATE MY SOUTHERNNESS AND be able to fully acknowledge my blackness until I left my hometown of Albany, Georgia, to go to work on my master's degree in Bloomington, Indiana. Before Indiana University, I couldn't tell you where Bloomington, let alone Indiana, was without a map. The only thing vaguely familiar about IU at the time was that my honors director, Ontario Wooden, went there for his doctorate, and that I'd been told stories by older folks at my church who said IU was where a lot of Southern Black folk went to pursue degrees when Southern schools pushed to stay segregated.

But I trusted Ontario: he was a 'Bany boy. His people knew my people. He had my best interests at heart.

Like most college seniors at the time, I was trying to figure out my next move after graduation. My grandparents were adamant about graduate school and I wanted to stay in the South. I had a boyfriend and wanted to stay nearby (because, priorities). I applied to Georgia and Florida schools. As usual, I posted up in the honors office where Ontario worked. I browsed his library. Ontario's office had a library that he let me peruse on the regular. Topics on all Black everything—Black political thought, Black history, Black educational history, pedagogy, and hip hop. Unless the door was closed, I bounced in with a casual "What's happenin', doc?" as I ran my finger against the spines of the books on the shelves. I memorized titles and quickly recognized when a book was new. We then commenced to talk about the topic of the day, often graduate school and my plans after Albany State.

"Miss Barnett, you're working on graduate applications, correct?"

I was only half paying attention, looking at the new books. "Yup. Almost done, doc. Submitting to Georgia State, Georgia, Florida State…" I picked up a book and pointed it at him. "Is this book new?"

Ontario poked the air, quickly pointing his index finger at me and motioning to sit down in the chair in front of his desk. "Hold up. All of those schools are in the South."

"And?"

"Close the door, Ms. Barnett." Aw hell. Closing the door meant he was about to switch from Dr. Wooden to Ontario, the one fluent in Albanese, the 'Bany boy.

"Lil' Girl, why you casting your net so close? Get the hell out of the South," he said.

I shrugged. "Ain't nothing wrong with staying in the South, doc."

I moved to the South permanently in 1998, where my grandparents saved me from myself and loved me back whole. I found myself in the music, the food, the people. I was a Down South Georgia Girl who loved OutKast and Trap music. I healed in the South. It hadn't been nothing but good to me. It was comforting to know my community would love me and keep me from the brink. I was comfortable. And in love with the scenery and my future husband, Roy.

Ontario didn't care.

"They're not going to pay for your degree. Expand your boundaries! Apply to Indiana. Maybe Ohio State. Get your ass out of the South. It will always be here. Come back after you get some different perspective."

I applied and got accepted into the African American and African Diaspora Studies program at Indiana University Bloomington. Gina Mae was leaving the South. *For real leaving the South*. Roy helped me pack my shit and I was out.

. . .

We drove the full eighteen hours from the 'Bany to Bloomington. We listened through his CD book and my CD book at least twice. Cee-Lo Green, OutKast, Goodie Mob, T.I., and Young Jeezy rapped us along the way. I munched on some of my Nana's good cooking, like fried fatback, biscuits, and sweet tea. I felt like I was on the Underground Railroad at some points of the trip, the car being guided through misty back roads by our headlights and the elongated shadows of trees that looked primed for nooses.

"This is some creepy shit," Roy said.

I nodded in agreement.

We arrived the day of my orientation. With a quick peck on the cheek, I left Roy to unpack my stuff and left to meet my cohort. During conversations between orientation sessions, we received words to live by:

There's no Black radio here. You got satellite, right?

Get used to the looks you'll get from your white students if you are TA'ing.

Don't stop at any of the small towns outside of Bloomington after sundown.

Sundown towns? Word? What fresh hell had I gotten myself into?

But I really knew I was out of the South when I realized that neither Bloomington nor IU had a goddamn Popeyes. How the hell do you call yourself a diverse institution of higher learning without a Popeyes? The KFC up the street from my apartment only gave me a box of bubble guts.

My hopes were dashed again when I saw a Waffle House, but not *that* Waffle House with a sign to let you know they didn't make their hash browns scattered or smothered. Out of pure respect for the Black and yellow sign, I refused to try their waffles. Even worse, Bloomington didn't play OutKast's new movie *Idlewild*. Pulling my Southern and Black folk card at the same time? Jesus be a spicy chicken strip box.

No Popeyes, no *Idlewild*, no Black music station, no touchstones of Black familiarity. I was OutKasted, alright.

It was official. I was out of the jurisdictions of Georgia and my Down South Georgia Girl familiarity. I was in the land of snow, sundown towns, and the Klan. Literally. I was in Bloomington when the Ku Klux Klan marched downtown in my second semester of graduate school. I'd never had to deal with the Klan directly. I went straight to the source who did: Paw Paw. When I called home, I usually just spoke to my Nana Boo while Paw Paw hollered hello in the background. This time was different.

"Hey Paw Paw! How you?"

"Hey, dea' sweetness! I'm good. What's going on up there in Indiana?"

"Paw Paw, they have a Klan rally today. A Klan rally!"

I heard a rumbling, possibly Paw Paw changing

hands or gripping the receiver, and a few deep breaths on the other end of the receiver.

"Paw Paw?"

"You stay inside the house," Paw Paw commanded. He had a bit of extra bass in his voice. That meant he was being dead serious. "Do not leave the house. You hear me? Do NOT leave the house," he repeated.

"Yes, sir," I said.

Paw Paw's voice was strained but adamant. He was speaking from a dark memory. His father pissed off a member of the Klan and they were out for my great-grandfather's blood. Paw Paw told me they had to run from their house in the middle of the night to stay safe. I have no doubt that his jaw was tight with inherited tension and his concern for my safety.

"Stay in the house and call us later this evening to let us know you are okay," he demanded.

"Yes, sir," I said.

Living in Bloomington made it apparent there were two types of racism: that "us-is" racism from the South and that "accidental" racism up North. In the South, Black and white folks straight up told or indicated to your Black ass they didn't like you because you were Black. A clutched purse. A quick round of "Dixie" and a raggedy Old Glory shirt wishing for the good ole days of Southern pride and slavery. A "kill yo-self" glare. A casually dropped racial slur among friends. A forcefully dropped one among acquaintances. There's no need to second guess if someone is anti-Black.

Bloomington, however, was filled with accidental racists. Folks who accidentally got caught doing racist shit. The kind of folks that dropped your class and accidentally got overheard that the reason they dropped your class was because you were Black. The ones that smiled in your face in class and said, "Appreciate your passion for Black culture," but behind closed doors suggested for you to reconsider graduate studies because your writing skills were not up to par to non-historically-Black and regionally accredited schools. Then there was the white guy who thought of himself as "accidentally white": the "I'm every human" white dude who was all-lives-matter before it was a thing. The guy, let's call him Saul, who said he only saw the humanity of others and depicted himself as a "Kum Bah Yah" Jesus. Saul, the human rights advocate who cut off the Black women in class to say he disagreed. Saul, the guy who still claimed his ex-Brazilian wife and chuckled at being mistaken for being Brazilian because he knew how to say Paulo Freire. And then there was the fateful day Saul suffered a shocked and cracked face: he took his overzealous cultural missionary spiel a step too far because he called the Black girl from South Georgia "over-passionate" in her ideas about Black people. The Black girl from South Georgia informed Saul she gave a fat fuck about the time he spent in XYZ-onia with Negroids and to mind his business cause she ain't the one. Ever.

. . .

But then was that one time, that one time that old racism blended with fresh complicity. It was dark and I was walking to my car after buying soda and 10-for-$10 ramen for the week because graduate school money was short and I needed to stretch it. Then I saw Ole Boy, the one Black boy from my class. I gave him a quick smile and a slow nod. He smiled and gave a quick wave.

I kept it moving because the bottles were heavy and it was cold outside. I happened to turn around and see dude from the Kroger's manager board blasting Ole Boy for putting something in his pockets. He threatened Ole Boy with police and being arrested. Ole Boy forcefully and adamantly defended his honor with a tart *"I ain't got SHIT in my pockets!"*

I blinked.

Ole Boy looked at me for confirmation of his innocence. I didn't know if Ole Boy had something in his pockets or not, but I got his back. I took a step closer. Manager dude turned red as he caught me mean-mugging the shit outta him. Ole Boy's hands were still tightly clasping his pockets. Manager Dude insisted Ole Boy empties his pockets.

Ole Boy started to crumble and fidget. I started to feel queasy.

I wanted to scream, STAY UP, OLE BOY! STAY UP, NIGGA! But the words lodged in my throat. They burned.

Slowly, Ole Boy emptied his pockets. He looked defeated. I felt sick. Ole Boy looked at me as I fumbled with my keys trying not to cry.

Ain't shit in that man's pockets.

Manager Dude mumbled some bullshit line. "Oh. I was following up with another employee that said…" I zoned out as his punk ass scurried back into the Kroger.

I wanted to go raise hell and read Manager Dude for filth. But I just stood there disgusted. With my complicit ass. I stood there dumbfounded and ashamed. Ole Boy was still looking at me. ⊚

Dysplasia

Natalia Sylvester

I GREW UP NOT ASKING MANY QUESTIONS. I thought all children had something that made their bodies different: my sister had her allergy shots, I had my hip problem.

"I'm having an operation tomorrow," I told a dry cleaning attendant on the eve of my first surgery in the United States. It felt exciting to me, in the way that getting ice cream is exciting to a six-year-old, each flavor promising a new experience, each new experience an adventure. I remember my mom gently shushing me. It wasn't out of shame, but perhaps for want of privacy. The morning of my surgery, she dressed me in a brand-new outfit—a black skirt, white blouse with red polka dots, white ruffled socks, and shiny vinyl shoes. We took a picture, her and my father, in our apartment living room. When I flip through our old photo albums, I remember the moment vividly, how ecstatic I was, but the deathly fear on their faces is something I never noticed until now.

That's the thing about being an immigrant, a child of immigrants: you learn not to over-interrogate the past. You sense your questions are unanswerable, because asking them means you're questioning the path your parents took, and you do not want to be another voice, like their own, that casts doubt. You learn to listen to the silences, to glean your truths from the unspoken. Revelations make their way to you nonchalantly, years and years later, in ordinary moments, and you nod as if this information is nothing new, as if you hadn't been searching for it all along.

The first words I ever spoke in English were not mine. I was four, and my family hadn't even been in the United States a year when my mom took me to see an orthopedic surgeon at Miami Children's Hospital.

On the drive over she handed me a silver figurine, no taller than a can of Coke. It was sculpted in the shape of a llama, or perhaps it was a cathedral—I know with certainty it was one of the two, because in Peru, these are typical gifts, small tokens given to others as if to say, *Here is a part of us and our culture.*

Repeat after me, my mother said. "This is for you, Dr. King."

This is for you, Dr. King.

Again, and again, until I'd committed the words to memory, until they were sounds I could sing without understanding them. I practiced my piece with arms outstretched, both hands holding my offering as if it were a heavy stone rather than thin sheets of precious metal.

Given his name, I imagined my doctor as a regal, authoritarian figure, someone capable of great power and benevolence. He and so many others gained my trust implicitly as my family moved from state to state throughout the 90s: the doctor in Gainesville, Florida, who was dressed as a witch on the Halloween afternoon we first met, when I was nine. The surgeon from San Antonio, who everyone in McAllen, Texas, insisted was the best, who we had to wait months to see when I was eleven because he only visited the Rio Grande Valley twice a year. The good friend of my uncle's, a Haitian American surgeon who last operated on me at fourteen, in a typically two-hour procedure that took six. It turned out the renowned San Antonio doctor had told us all looked good, no further treatment was necessary, when he should have operated on me years ago.

I was born with a problem on my left hip. Throughout childhood, this was the language I had to explain it, which makes sense, because how do you tell a one, two, three, six-year-old, why her body is always needing to be fixed, why the surgeries come one after the other after the other, without admitting there is something just slightly off?

The way the doctors always explained it was by balling one hand into a fist and covering it with the other. This was a healthy hip in its socket. Then they'd slide the fist under their palm and fingers, until the fingertips were barely holding on to the knuckles, until it looked like at any moment, the head of the hip could just slip out of its socket. This was my hip. Solving the problem of its displacement meant braces and casts, screws and hardware drilled in and out of my femur, crutches and walkers and wheelchairs.

"You'll be able to feel the rain coming," is what Dr. King once told me, but being six, I didn't understand what he meant—that arthritic joints ache when the barometric pressure in the air shifts before the rain falls, that some people can sense the weather in their bones. Instead I pictured it as a super power, my body triumphing over the weather report. I couldn't have imagined that what he described, with such glee that I practically wished for it, was pain.

In the end it didn't matter, because I never felt the rain. Or perhaps I always felt it and didn't know the difference. Nearly every day in Miami, it showers, and when it doesn't the humidity looms, a thick coat over your skin. My body didn't have a barometer for what was a normal amount of discomfort.

The actual term for what I have is developmental dysplasia of the hip. Sometimes they call it dislocation. Caught early enough in babies it's easily rectified with a harness that holds the joint in place for one to two months. My case turned out to be different, in the way that all bodies are different, in the way that science can often explain how but not why.

The narrative I know is this: In Peru, I had a series of surgeries before I turned one. When we moved to the United States, I had four more: one in first grade, another in third, fourth, and ninth. My final surgery is somewhere in a certain future, the one doctors have always told me I'll need when I'm in my forties, when my hip will just finally need to be replaced.

Soon after my first book came out in 2014, my mom started decluttering her home. Each trip back to Miami yielded a new box of books and photos, files and documents that she thought I might want to keep. Once, she handed me a giant manila folder stuffed with all my x-rays from the time I was a baby. Numbers and figures scribbled on the films by doctors told me a story I already knew, of how displacement had spread from my hips to my legs, causing a half-inch difference between them, and to my spine, which has scoliosis of about eleven degrees.

What you don't see on the bones you see on my skin: three scars, varying in length from two to ten inches. The countless ways I tried hiding them growing up—arms rigid against my hip when I wore a bathing suit, hands clutching my chair whenever I sat down and my shorts rode up to expose the former wounds. There are the taunts of children who didn't understand why a little girl would walk with a limp, who felt the need to laugh as they imitated my unique cadence. And there is the teenager who lived in our apartment complex in Gainesville, who'd never looked twice at this eight-year-old girl but who proclaimed, loud enough for all the other kids at the pool to hear, that my scar was so cool. I remember that kindness most of all.

Documentation provides facts yet so often fails truth. But it is all there, in my bones, skin, body, memory. Dysplasia is not just how I was born but how I've lived, and it's taken me years to finally feel at home here, within this body and this hip that has survived so much, that has taught me strength is not never being hurt. Strength is fighting, recovering, healing, enduring. It is navigating the world when we have no maps, just a skeleton of a journey we hope will protect our hearts.

Two years ago, my mom gave me a plastic bag filled with old pictures of my father's side of the family and my first Peruvian passport. In it, I'm maybe six months old. The black-and-white square picture is a study in contrasts. White, overflowing dress. Black, wide eyes. Flipping through it, I expected to find evidence of when we first moved to the United States in 1988. Instead I found a stamp from '85.

This is the first office visit for this 7mo. old female seen at this time for evaluation concerning the lower extremities.

"We came here before we moved?" I asked.

"You and I did. To see Dr. King."

Before we came for a better life, we came hoping for better care.

Later, I would find Dr. King's notes in a manila folder my mother gave me, labeled *natalia's medical records* in pencil. Pages of operative reports, post-op reports, and radiology consultations have slowly begun to fill in the gaps between my own knowledge of my body and my doctors'. On a treatment record dated March 1, 1994, the day my cast was removed six-weeks post-surgery, my physical therapist wrote, *the patient is very anxious/hesitant concerning left knee movements.*

They recorded status. I remember the ache. Minutes after my cast was removed, with my leg stiff and atrophied, my knee unable to bend from the position it'd held for the last forty-two days, an x-ray technician placed me on a metal table and pushed my leg taut against the cold surface without even a hint of a warning. That one forced movement caused the greatest pain I'd ever felt, before and since then. I kept quiet through all of it, afraid to give voice to the pain or betray the silent plea of my first English words in this country.

"This is for you, Dr. King."

Here is a part of me. Take good care of it, be kind.

Soon after my mom gave me my old passport, I finally felt the weather. It was a cold, drizzly day in Austin and the drops of precipitation had seeped through my jacket and into my hip. It was a tightness, a slowing of all the particles inside and outside of me. It hurt but it also meant that I hadn't been hurting before, and it passed just as quickly as it arrived. Since then, it's happened again—rarely, but enough for me to understand the language of my body. Enough for me to ask and give myself what it needs.

A couple of winters ago, I sprained my knee during a workout and found myself, at thirty-three, seeing an orthopedic surgeon for something other than my hip for the first time in my life. The doctor examined my x-rays before seeing me, so when he came into the examination room the first words he said were, "You have a bad hip, but you already knew that."

I wanted to tell him no. This hip that I have is good. For years we cut into it, drilled holes and screws into its marrow. It healed for me. It became strong for me. It is my flesh, my bone, my skeleton on which all that I am, all I ever grew to become, still stands. ◉

White Devil in Blue:
Duke Basketball, Religion, and
Modern Day Slavery in the "New" South

Christena Cleveland

AT THE TIPOFF, THE BALL SPIRALED TO THE OTHER
team, and the Duke Blue Devils immediately scrambled into a full court press.

"Oh my god," I cringed.

Duke was the heavy favorite, and full court presses—aggressive, frenetic defensive strategies that are designed to discombobulate the other team and force them into making a mistake—are typically reserved for even match-ups or late in the game when the score is close.

Why begin *this game with a full court press*? I wondered. *That seems kind of cruel. Maybe Duke really* is *the Evil Empire.*

A lifelong college basketball fan, this wasn't my first NCAA game. But as a new faculty member at Duke University's Divinity School, it was my first Blue Devils game. A representative from the school's advancement office had asked me to accompany him and a prospective donor to the game. My transition to Duke had been excruciating, and only a few months in, I was already exhausted. But since the donor's gift would potentially offer much-needed funds for my research, I agreed to attend the game. It wasn't until I arrived at Duke's famed Cameron Indoor Stadium and learned *who* Duke was playing that I began to regret my decision.

In the fall of 2015, the Duke Blue Devils were the reigning NCAA Division 1 Men's Basketball Champions. Their opponents were the Livingstone College Blue Bears. New to the South, I had never heard of Livingstone College—but upon googling it, I learned that the Division II Blue Bears had only won about half their games the previous season.

The Blue Bears were about to get their asses whooped and I felt sorry for them.

But the knot didn't begin to form in my gut until I scrolled through Livingstone's website and learned something else about the school: it's an HBCU founded by the African Methodist Episcopal Zion church.

Oh my god, I thought to myself as I simultaneously found my seat, greeted the donor, and read up on Livingstone's history. "The Blue Bears are about to get their *Black* asses whooped."

That's why I couldn't help but cringe when I witnessed the mostly-white Blue Devils attack the all-Black Blue Bears with a full court press right from the start. I half-heartedly made small talk with the white donor, but my Black mind and body trembled as my ongoing Google search uncovered more details about Livingstone.

Oh my god. This tiny, 700-student HBCU is facing off against the mighty, 16,000-student Duke University.

Oh my god. Livingstone College is a severely under-resourced institution that perennially struggles to meet its budget while Duke is swimming in a vast pool of money.

Oh my god. Livingstone's graduation rate is only 24%. Only a resource vacuum could produce a statistic that dismal.

Oh my god. The African Methodist Episcopal denomination that founded Livingstone exists because the white Methodists did not allow Black people to fully participate in their churches.

Oh my god. The Black Methodists founded Livingstone College for Black students because white Methodist schools like Duke did not allow Black students.

Oh my god. The Black Methodist Blue Bears are about to get their asses whooped by the white Methodist Blue Devils.

. . .

As I pieced the puzzle together, I recognized that on one level, what was happening on the court was a classic case of David versus Goliath. The NCAA preseason, in which teams from different leagues and divisions often play each other, is rife with such cases. I knew this because I grew up around high-stakes college basketball. The man I lovingly call my godfather coached the great Cal Berkeley teams of the 1990s, including teams led by NBA stars Jason Kidd and Shareef Abdur-Rahim. My interactions with my godfather and his colleagues exposed me to the business side of the game, and I learned that poor schools often agree to play preseason games against rich schools because the income from one such game keeps their entire athletic department afloat for a year. The power inequity between poor schools and rich schools is so great and so immovable that poor teams endure annual beatings by rich teams in order to receive a much-needed paycheck.

This game between Duke and Livingstone was no different; the Blue Bears' ass whooping at the hands of the Blue Devils was a necessary condition of their survival. Yet what glaringly stood out to me as a newcomer to the South were the racial and religious power dynamics at play in this particular game. This particular game occurred at a predominantly-white institution that was funded by income made possible through African slavery. This particular game occurred on a prosperous campus full of buildings honoring Methodist slaveholders, such as Carr Hall, which was named after major Duke donor, white Methodist, and slaveholder Julian Carr. He publicly boasted of "horse-whipping" Black women. It was in this specific historical and social context that the *Black* Methodist Blue Bears received their own modern-day horse-whipping from the *white* Methodist Blue Devils.

More than a classic case of David versus Goliath, this match-up was a classic case of Enslaved versus Slaveholder.

Just a stone's throw away, conspicuously situated among the Christian saints that line the entrance to Duke's opulent gothic chapel—stood a life-size statue of Robert E. Lee. His prominent presence at the center of Duke religious life silently declared a holy benediction on the modern-day horse-whipping occurring over on the basketball court.

Having just taught a course on Malcolm X, I immediately thought of his definition of a white devil: "Unless we call one white man, by name, a 'devil,' we are not speaking of any *individual* white man. We are speaking of the *collective* white man's *historical* record." [1]

When the collective history remains unatoned, the white devil lives on. It lives on in the Methodist church's unwillingness to reckon with its racist past and present. It lives on in confederate monuments all over the South. It lives on in racial discrepancies among graduation rates. It lives on at stupid-rich Duke while financially-fraught HBCUs suffer just a

1 The Autobiography of Malcolm X, p. 306

few miles down the road. It lives on in this basketball game, in which the embodied souls of Black boys must endure a beating in order for their college to survive another year. It lives on in Duke Blue.

Trapped in my own thoughts, I only looked up at the game when the crowd cheered because someone had just scored. Not surprisingly, the mostly-white Blue Devils did most of the scoring, as the Black Blue Bears toiled under Duke's ruthless attack. But once in a while a Black Blue Bear would score—and when that happened, I couldn't help but cheer wildly. My instinctual pro-Blackness could not be suppressed.

The white donor, who had the money I needed in order to be successful at Duke, repeatedly glanced at me, surveilling my unabashed support of Livingstone. Just before halftime, he leaned toward me and whispered into my ear, "*I see you.* I see you cheering for the other team." His remark was a warning, a reminder that he held the key to my success and that he was watching me.

It also reinforced the truth that though I was an "invited guest" sitting in the stands, I was no different than the Black Blue Bears on the court. We were all niggers on the same plantation. They were field niggers, toiling under the brutal whip on the court. I was a house nigger, under surveillance in the Big House, required to play a role in order to maintain my "special status." As long as I didn't identify with the field niggers on the court, I could remain in the stands and retain access to the slavery-endowed bounty of Duke. As long as I didn't speak up about the living, breathing white devil in blue, I would never find myself in a resource vacuum like Livingstone College.

The white donor's words were simply a reinforcement because I had learned this lesson in a visceral way just two weeks prior to the game. In a one-on-one meeting with my Dean, I naively shared my unfiltered concerns about the overwhelming institutional racism at Duke Divinity School, and how I believed it was negatively impacting my transition as a new Black faculty member as well as the transitions of the new Black students. Like the white Blue Devils, the Dean responded right off the bat with a full court press. She leaned forward in her throne-like chair, stared me in the eye and said, "You know, some people just aren't cut out to be faculty at Duke Divinity School. It sounds like you're one of them. I want to give you permission to leave."

In the Dean's office that day, I kept my mouth shut. Like the poor basketball teams who have endured a trouncing by the rich teams in order to stay alive, I endured the Dean's whipping. And during the second half of the game, I made a concerted effort to cheer for the white Blue Devils as they horse-whipped the Black Blue Bears. The white donor was pleased with my performance, and at the end of the game he agreed to help fund my research project.

After the game, I returned to my office to put in

a few more hours of work. As I walked by Duke chapel on my way to the divinity school, Robert E. Lee mocked me in the blue moonlight. White devil in blue, indeed. ◉

Southern, Not a Belle

Nichole Perkins

WHEN I FIRST STARTED USING ONLINE DATING profiles, away from my Nashville home, I'd include I was Southern in my "About Me" section. I'm proud of being raised in the South, but after conversations with several matches started off in the same manner, I realized I needed to clarify some things. I may be Southern, but I am nobody's belle.

Like most people, when I'm home, my accent is more relaxed; my speech patterns and mannerisms reflect the culture that raised me. Sometimes that means I talk too fast and make sounds that feel like words yet aren't. Anyone five years older than I am is a ma'am or sir. My voice is a little higher and more childlike because when I'm home, surrounded by family, I feel permanently eight years old. That's not a bad thing. I've come to appreciate it and let my mother tease me because I know she misses me more than she can say. But when I'm away from home, unless you're paying a particular kind of attention, it may be hard to tell where I'm from, just by the way I talk. My codeswitch game is real. I'm one of those people who absorb colloquialisms and other people's accents while talking to them, so after living in New Orleans, Los Angeles, the D.C. area, and now Brooklyn, my phrasing can be all over the place.

When I go on dates, I often hear, "You don't sound like you're from the South." The men color their comments with a blend of disappointment and surprise. They expect to hear the exaggerated accent from film and television. They want to laugh at my accent and offer me words to hear how I pronounce them. My accent is not a parlor trick. Does that syrupy-thick drawl really exist? Absolutely. Do I have it? Well, I'm no Scarlett O'Hara, but every now and then something close comes out, but whatever kind of accent I have, it's not going to appear on a first date, not when I'm trying to make sure my companion is not about to serial-kill me. I'm too tense to let much of the real me out.

These first dates or first few texts via dating apps always make it clear that the men on the other side of me not only expect a particular sound to come from my mouth, but also a particular kind of subservience. What makes that so peculiar is the idea that a Southern belle is a doormat, someone who's supposed to fetch a man's slippers and never question him. This is how I know these Yankee men have no clue what a real Southern belle is beyond a dainty femme with a twang.

The myth of the Southern belle was created after the Civil War, and it wasn't so much to rebuild women's morale as to make sure people knew that Southern white women were of a certain upper class, even if they didn't have slaves anymore, according to Giselle Roberts in her article "The Confederate Belle: The Belle Ideal, Patriotic Womanhood, and Wartime Reality in Louisiana and Mississippi, 1861-1865," originally published by the Louisiana Historical Association. "In the postbellum South, ladies…continued to cling to the preexisting racial and class hierarchy as they looked for ways to assert their elite status in a world without wealth or slaves," Roberts claims. The Southern belle is a woman who doesn't lift a finger. Someone else, previously enslaved, tends to her needs. She is educated enough to make witty conversation but not enough to challenge a man. She is as innocent as the first snowfall and only suffers through her husband's lovemaking for the purpose of having children because a real lady would never enjoy sex. It's too rough for her delicate disposition. All of this is in direct opposition to the ways Black women, enslaved and then freed, were maligned. Black women worked and did not have fine clothes, servants, or education. Their "innocence" was often taken from them without their consent. White Southern belles were positioned as being too delicate while Black women, as enslaved or freed, were considered fair game to men's sexual desires, something Harriet Jacobs referred to as living in "an atmosphere of licentiousness and fear," in her slave narrative *Incidents in the Life of a Slave Girl*. A Southern belle wasn't something that really existed until it was called into being as part of racist propaganda.

When I first moved to Brooklyn in January 2017, I began dating a man I nicknamed Casually Racist Charlie. (Becoming involved with him was a mistake, based in loneliness and boredom, but I figured I'd get some good stories out of the brief relationship). We had met via a dating app and during our text exchanges, he commented on my "Southern" bio. I told him I was from Tennessee, and Casually Racist Charlie immediately responded, "Oh! Does that mean I've got a Southern belle on my hands?" I'm glad he couldn't see me roll my eyes. Non-Southern men ask me that almost every time I say where I'm from. The history of the term "Southern belle" is too loaded for me to take lightly, although I never explain in great detail why I'm not a Southern belle. I just smile and say, "No. I'm not much of a lady." Sometimes the discussion goes on from there, and sometimes the flirting takes over. I am not a lady, so whatever happens after that will not be because of polite obligation, but because of my assertive choice.

When I date in the South or even Southern men who've moved away from home, they see me as more than just a Southern femme fantasy. I let my accent break free and I am a little sweeter. I pay more careful attention to a Southern man's flattery. It feels much more like worship. Southern men have such elaborate compliments. One night, I'd made an eggplant lasagna and my vegetarian then-boyfriend from Virginia asked me, after he'd inhaled two plates of the stuff, if I had put my...well, my very special, private place in the dish to make it taste so good. What a filthy sweet bit of praise that was! Only something a Southern man could come up with. It still makes me preen a bit to think about it.

When I'm away from the South or dating a non-Southern man, the man seems to go to extremes to prove he doesn't care about me, that I should work to impress him. I dated a man from the Bay Area in California who refused to give compliments, explaining he wasn't good at them and didn't think they were necessary. Southern men are effusive with compliments, sometimes to the point of disbelief. In my experience, Southern men love to heap praise on their women. Making their women feel good is a point of pride, I think. Don't get me wrong. I've been a victim of street harassment and called horrible names for rejecting someone's advances no matter where I was in the country, but at home, it seems like men approach me more carefully more often than not. In the South, a man will offer to fill my tank at the gas station in exchange for my number or he'll try to have an actual conversation with me. Twice, when I lived in Los Angeles, men approached me during visits to the grocery store as if I were a sex worker and asked how much I cost. Another Los Angeles man accosted me at a bus stop.

When I visit my Nashville home, depending on the length of my stay, I usually take my brother to the barber shop. I secretly love this errand, even though it's not very feminist of me. Yes, it's a way for me and my brother to have some quality time together away from the house, but, to be honest, I love the fall of silence when I enter the shop. Perhaps because I don't go to barber shops on a regular basis, I don't feel the same kind of dread my mother or my friends do when they go. The barber shop is considered a place of sacred masculinity, especially in Black American communities, and sometimes that means harassing women dropping off their sons. I know this, and yet, when I go home, the barber shop makes me feel powerful and seen in a way I don't feel outside of the South.

Away from the South, it feels like men see me as a collection of stereotypes they're supposed to laugh at, no matter how liberal and progressive they claim to be, especially when compared to life below the Mason-Dixon line. At home, I'm the kind of woman men have been told to make a wife, so the cat calls are "Hey, miss lady" or a constant stream of "Ma'am! Ma'am! Miss!" until they realize I'm ignoring them. When I'm home, the sense of familiarity makes me feel less threatened if I smile to be polite. Southern hospitality is a real thing, and I do have manners. Don't get me wrong, but I'm not foolish enough to relax completely around strange men trying to holler at me on the street or at the grocery store. There's only so far Southern charm can take you.

Dating has enough challenges without people adding in outdated gender expectations and regional stereotypes. I live in Brooklyn now. When I tell men I'm Southern and they ask about being a belle or ask me to say certain words, I roll my eyes. There are some words I cannot say without my Tennessee sweetness sticking to them. I try to avoid them, not out of shame, but to avoid the assumptions and the silly script men want to play out. I'm the other kind of Southern belle: direct and full of fire. I will not play coy. I will not play stupid. If you pull my accent out of me, it's in a moment of comfort and passion, and you should be honored.

I miss the way men see me when I'm back in the South, and I don't just mean I miss the way men flirt with me. It's easy to dismiss the way I'm treated back home as a part of our famed Southern hospitality, but it seems more than that. Away from the South, I become invisible. On the streets, people walk into me like I'm glass. My dating life is a series of dissatisfying swipes and matched conversations that fade quickly. Men seem to prepare themselves for a caricature, and when they realize I am a real person, they don't know how to go from there. Yet when I am home, I stop conversations. People say *excuse me* if they bump into me. Men smile with all their teeth at the sight of me. ◉

White, Other, and Black

Ivelisse Rodriguez

"OH, WAIT, I'M NOT WHITE," I SAID, PARTIALLY amused. After all, I was stating the obvious to the woman at the DMV who had me verify my license and voter registration information. "Isn't there a Hispanic/ Latino category?" I asked even though that seemed like another silly thing to say. I mean, there had to be a Hispanic/Latino (person of Cuban, Mexican, Puerto Rican, South or Central American, or other Spanish culture or origin regardless of race) box to check off.

"No," she said.

"No?"

"No," she reaffirmed.

My mother had gone to the DMV the day before in Clayton, North Carolina, and hadn't mentioned this racial/ethnic conundrum. And partly due to my exaggerated stereotypes of the South, I believed the woman at the DMV and thought, well, this is the South.

"Wait, so what do the other Latinos pick?" I asked, genuinely curious.

She leaned forward and said in a hushed conspiratorial tone, "They usually pick white."

"What? Really?" I was stunned and perplexed by this admission. In terms of Latinos in North Carolina, they are mostly Mexican or Mexican-American. And not the blue-eyed, blonde-haired Mexicans of telenovelas. So definitely not white. But not Black either.

I assumed she marked "white" by accident, but she had checked it off on purpose based on past experience. Yet, I was still curious as to why she defaulted to white versus Black when she looked at me. I had grown up my whole life with the sensibility that I am a dark-skinned Puerto Rican. Where I grew up, in Holyoke, Massachusetts, that was one of two identifiers for Puerto Ricans—the other one was light-skinned. And no Puerto Rican would ever call me the latter.

But I was in North Carolina now, and while there are some Puerto Ricans and Dominicans here, we don't have large enough populations or lengthy histories in the region that would allow us to be easily recognizable or identifiable. So maybe it was reasonable that Latinxs, especially Caribbean Latinxs—a multiracial group of people who normally define themselves as a mix of Indigenous, African, and Spanish ancestry would perplex someone. We come in a thousand colors and configurations of hair texture and facial features. My mother is frequently mistaken for Filipino. My sister is usually assumed to be African American. Depending upon where I am and how I wear my hair, I've been asked if I am Dominican, Cape Verdean, Cuban, or Indian. These were all reasonable assumptions, though. White, however, was really far-fetched and out of the realm of possibility.

To me, the South was a place of slavery, the one-drop rule, Jim Crow laws. In other words, some reified image that in all likelihood no longer reflected the South of today. I laughed and said, "Yeah, I don't think that I can show up to a voting booth in North Carolina with voter registration information that says I'm white. So put down Black."

The DMV is normally wretched, but the DMV in Clayton, North Carolina, was small and orderly—less than thirty people either waited or worked there. This was as close as you could get to a pleasant experience at the DMV, so I felt at ease chatting up the petite, older Black woman in glasses who was having a hard time figuring out how to classify me.

She clacked on her keyboard and her printer whirred. She handed me the form, still warm from the machine. Ready to get out of there, and with my pen poised in the air, I saw she had chosen "Other". My biggest concern before coming to the DMV was whether or not I could pass the eye exam (I did!), but now I was thrown into a racial/ethnic tug-of-war.

"Other" was a step up from "white". We were getting warmer. "No, no. I want you to put down Black," I said, insistent, passing the form back to her. During this back and forth, I was reminded of sociologist Clara E. Rodriguez's ideas about the negotiations Latinxs have to make around trying to fit into the US racial classification system when they fill out census forms. When race is a requirement, Latinxs don't always know what category to slot themselves into because they are trying to fit into rigid racial identities that are disparate from how they categorize themselves.

In Holyoke, I was clearly Puerto Rican. It is not the first place you would ever expect Puerto Ricans, but we make up forty-four percent of the population, and unbeknownst to the whole world, we have the largest concentration of Puerto Ricans outside of Puerto Rico. We have a history in the city and the region that dates back to the 1950s when the Puerto Ricans went to Holyoke and neighboring cities in Western Massachusetts to work in the tobacco fields. With this history and with a large population, I don't think I was ever confused for anything other than what I really was.

When outside of Holyoke, other people didn't always know how to categorize me, but I knew where I fit. While others' view of me was situational, it was always fixed for me. And to me (and other Puerto Ricans and Latinxs), I'm a dark-skinned Puerto Rican, so if we were all going to have to choose between these three options (white, other, and Black), my fellow Latinxs and I would have agreed upon Black as the best choice here.

The woman at the DMV was flustered. "But if your information says you are Black when you go vote, then they are going to think you are *Black*," she said as she rubbed her skin.

"African American?" I asked.

She nodded.

Ah, so here was her real issue. Because we were in the South, Black solely meant African American. I was in a place where Blackness had a significant history that was tied to centuries of slavery, Jim Crow, lynching, and to a specific group of Black people who eventually became African American. My previous assumption that my Blackness was obvious was in some ways incorrect, not only because of the dearth of history and community of Puerto Ricans in the South but also because, here, Black historically equaled African American. So the woman at the DMV assumed I was not African American, therefore, not Black.

What ensued was an engaging conversation about our different perceptions of Blackness. When I think Black, I think about a reference to color that is open to use for anyone from the African Diaspora. After studying Blackness in the US, the Spanish-speaking Caribbean, and Brazil, I didn't equate Blackness with a specific group of people. And after living in the New York City area and the Northeast, being Black did not mean you were necessarily African American. It could, but it wasn't the only possible option at the other end of the equal sign. Instead, some or all Panamanians, Jamaicans, Haitians, Nigerians, Colombians, Puerto Ricans, and a multitude of people from even more nations could be described as Black, but a Black wholly disassociated from its significance here in the US, because the meaning of Blackness is not fixed across the globe. It is a misnomer to assume that everyone who is Black is African American.

After I pled my case to the woman at the DMV, she reprinted the form and finally put Black down. While "Black" wasn't the whole story as it didn't convey my history and my people, it was as close as I was going to get that day at the DMV.

*Later, when I went home and recounted the whole story to my mother, she said, "Oh, there was a Hispanic/Latino category. That's what I checked off yesterday." ◉

Ain't Misbehaving

Gary Jackson

> *And fantasy it was, for we were not strong, only aggressive; we were not free, merely licensed; we were not compassionate, we were polite; not good, but well behaved.*
>
> —Toni Morrison, *The Bluest Eye*

WE WALKED DOWN KING STREET, THE MAIN downtown strip in Charleston, South Carolina, which is central to everything: the college, the college bars, the cheap eats, the tourist spots, the historic city market, The Battery, Louis Vuitton—everything. I was treating my mom and stepdad, both of whom had helped my wife and I drive a U-Haul from Albuquerque to Charleston to start my new job at the College of Charleston. But having only lived in the city for three days, I was still more tourist than native, and in fact would never be native, according to Charleston's standards: I was not from Charleston, nor my family or family's family. No surprise, then, that the three of us would stumble into Juanita Greenberg's Nacho Royale, lured by the promise of cheap tacos and even cheaper cold beer. It was late July and we were dying to get out of the sweltering heat. So different from the high desert nights I was used to in New Mexico, when even in the summer, after the sun went down, you could cool off by a good ten degrees.

Inside, we took note of the waitstaff—a collection of smiling young white women and men, and we compared them to what we glimpsed of the cooks in the kitchen, all of whom were Black and looking steadily down at the grill. *Huh*, my mother said, already working out a thesis. The food took so long, they comped us a meal—whether it was a good or bad omen, we couldn't decide. After dinner, we opted to walk around a little more and have another drink somewhere before going home.

My stepdad took note of all the bicycles hitched to light posts and scattered bike racks down side streets and near shopfronts, every one of them secured with student-priced twenty-dollar chains. *Niggas would've stole all these bikes back home*, my stepdad said. *Shit, I would clean up down here*. My mother laughed in agreement, but told him to be quiet since we were walking in public, and white folks were thick out tonight, as they are most nights on King Street. Of the few Black folks we saw, most of them were working in a kitchen or behind a counter.

I drove around for a while, partly because I didn't know how to hook onto I-26 to get back home, and partly because I wanted to prove my folks wrong— Charleston was just as Black as Dallas, Texas. Not that far north on King Street, near the I-26 entrance ramp, we drove by an apartment complex where a BBQ was in full swing. We saw thirty to forty Black folks chatting and lounging and kids popping wheelies on bikes. We smelled grilled and smoked meat. *There they are,* my stepdad smiled. *You can drop me off here.*

My mother is an expert at making snap decisions based off relatively limited information that usually work out for the best (see Exhibit A: my father), so I was fully prepared when she later confessed she felt something was *off* downtown. *They well-behaved down here,* she said, meaning the South, meaning she couldn't understand how people could just walk under the confederate flag's shadow on the state grounds, or walk by statues erected to honor pro-slavery seces-sionists on their way to school. I argued that just because we weren't stealing every unattended bike in Charleston, didn't necessarily mean anything either. Being *well-behaved* wasn't a sign of subservience. But I could see how the idea of the well-behaved Black man could be used against someone. Against me.

. . .

I've been teaching for roughly fifteen years. And during that time, I've amassed quite a few stories of teaching to a sea of white faces yearning for an English degree. Most of the more memorable stories happen exactly as you would expect: a student pushes against having to read about *so many Black poets* or confesses *these references would make more sense if I was Black, but since I'm not, I'm a little lost* or, my favorite, *what's a hot comb?* Any number of questions rooted part in genuine ignorance, part passive-aggression. These experiences aren't unique to Charleston. I've encountered those students, and will continue to encounter them for the rest of my life. And I usually respond with the assurance/reminder that these texts matter, that these writers matter. And I do it all with a smile, even when the occasional student uses my politeness against me.

It's no secret that my voice carries. My wife and I jokingly call this *Black man's voice* and joke about how long it took her to get used to it—the same voice I have used all my life. If my mother and I are in the same room, we do, in fact, shout at each other, so we can continue the conversation while one of us goes into another room to fix something to eat, use the bathroom, or turn on the TV. While standing in line to vote in the 2018 midterm election, I heard my name called out from someone standing about twelve people ahead of us in line. A coworker had picked me out after hearing me speak in what I thought was a low tone to my wife. People on the first floor of the English Department can hear my conferences with students in my fourth-floor office.

So I'm not surprised when I startle students when I call everyone's attention, when I tell a student this will be on the test, when I laugh out loud, when I yell hello from across campus. Once, a white male student accused me of always yelling, of always being angry. He even wrote in a midterm response paper that was supposed to focus on poetic form that he thought I had a *darkness* inside of me. I responded with concern for his well-being, as we are trained to do as professors who teach students who may be going through myriad issues in school or back home. But I was not about to explain or defend my own literal voice. Later, that same student submitted a poem for workshop in which he described a poetry class murdering their poetry professor then celebrating.

And did I modulate my voice? Try to consciously lower the register to hit right below that indecipherable decibel that made only white people uncomfortable but no one else? Of course I did. Look up the definition of well-behaved and there's a picture of an assistant professor trying to make tenure. Though I denied the student a direct apology, I thought back to what my mother said after only being in Charleston for three days: *They well-behaved down here.*

There are plenty of spaces where I'm hyper-aware that I'm being watched and assessed, where I am being viewed as an ambassador to Blackness, and someone says something that makes me want to bear my teeth and I have to decide how to respond. What do you do after a white man calls you Darius Rucker yet again in a bar? Then tells you when you do not immediately smile or laugh, *it's a compliment, you know*.

After a poetry reading, a well-meaning white woman told me, *It can't be that bad, can it?* I told her it was. *Maybe in Kansas,* she said, referencing one of my poems that I just read, *but here people don't act like that anymore.* I told her that I lived here, too, meaning Charleston, and also, the world. But she was already off and talking about something else, once again reminding me that I was not from here, and not part of her world. Or, more accurately, my world was considered invalid. *Just the other day, a Black man held the door open for me and my friends,* the woman said. I almost told her that Black man probably hated her guts, and that being polite did not equal forgiveness or grace. Maybe I should've said more, should've tried to explain. Instead, I simply finished my drink, thanked the organizers for putting the reading and reception together, and politely left. ◉

The Rich, Southern History of Black College Majorettes

Frederick McKindra

AS A BOY BACK IN ARKANSAS, WE CALLED THEM dancing girls—the all-female dance lines that combined the energy and precision of the high-step black college marching bands they fronted with lyrical, West African, jazz, contemporary, and hip-hop choreography. The result was almost too sexual to be looked upon straight on. I could only steal glances at the Golden Girls, the majorettes for the band at my father's alma mater, the University of Arkansas at Pine Bluff. I wasn't old enough to be leering at grown women like that, and why else would a boy be so transfixed by the dancers, unless of course he was "that way," one of the boys too femme to perform an authentic black masculinity—what folks back then called "sweet."

But you no longer have to be an initiate of Southern black college culture—the kin of some insufferably proud Southwestern Athletic Conference (SWAC) alumni; annual attendee to a black college classic or homecoming game; bystander at a local Juneteenth parade; nostalgist for TLC's "Baby-Baby-Baby" video, or NBC's *A Different World* or Spike Lee's *School Daze*—to recognize the style of dance performed by the majorettes fronting black college bands. To distinguish these auxiliary groups from more customary majorettes—women who march before traditional (white) bands twirling batons—some have begun calling these dancers "hip-hop majorettes." But that term is a recent invention and therefore anachronistic, a hastily applied umbrella description for a tradition of movement honed by these dance lines over the past half century.

In 2018, Houston-born pop star Beyoncé mined the black college majorette style for an iconic Coachella appearance with a phalanx of majorette-inspired dancers clearing the way for her, costumed as Nefertiti. This performance, along with an attendant Netflix concert film, *Homecoming*, arrived at an auspicious moment for majoretting. Advocates of this uniquely Southern performance style—a community that includes both Southern straight black women and femme gay black men—have been using digital media platforms throughout the 2010s to formalize and institutionalize the genre as a dance discipline. Beyoncé's 2018 Beychella performance served to culminate many cultural phenomena that have helped amplify the visibility of majorette dancers, including the emergence of commercial dance through televised dance competitions, the continued popularity of dance reality programming like Lifetime's *Bring It!* (which spawned a road tour that travels the South), and the work of amateur videographers who upload weekly game performance footage to YouTube, creating a digital archive of the dance form and making performances available for future study.

The black college majoretting style we know today began formally in the late '60s. Marching bands had long featured carnivalesque acts pulling acrobatic stunts or tossing and catching flaming batons as a part of their halftime entertainment, but dance lines enabled bands to dramatize the popular songs they were beginning to mine from the radio.

As the ability to watch black college bands was often limited to spectators attending live sporting events through the '60s, the claim made by Alcorn State University's Golden Girls to have originated contemporary black college majorette style through a televised performance at the 1968 Orange Blossom

Classic offers a tenuous origin date for today's majorettes, or "a featured squad with choreographed movements to an HBCU's marching band's live tunes," as the GGs define it. HBCU marching bands across the South quickly followed suit.

The Dancing Dolls of Southern University officially date back to 1969, founded by team adviser/coach Gracie Perkins and then-band director Isaac Greggs. The Dolls have enjoyed national acclaim due to the annual Bayou Classic in New Orleans, one of the few HBCU football games televised nationally today.

Jackson State University's J-Settes were founded in 1971, when Shirley Middleton, a former majorette and the squad's initial sponsor, petitioned for the majorettes to "put their batons down." Middleton, along with JSU twirler and choreographer Hollis Pippins, and eventual sponsor Narah Oatis, pioneered j-setting, a style of choreography distinguished by brusque movement originating in the pelvis and the stomping of a flat foot.

Traditionally, majorette fans choose between the more balletic style of the Southern University Dancing Dolls or the bawdier bucking of the J-Settes. The Dolls' style privileges fluidity in movement, a quality they describe as being poured "like milk." They are famous for their port de bras, or arcs made through the air with graceful, supported arms; slow body rolls; and struts and stand counts (eight counts of choreography performed and repeated in the stands of a stadium) which make them look like they are prancing and can be read as prissy.

If the Dolls pantomime seduction, then the J-Settes employ a style that is more explicit. J-Settes prefer grounded, flat-footed movement; they squat or bend or buck. To buck is to aggressively thrust the pelvis forward, a movement that is obviously sexually suggestive—and in the rubric of American sexuality, deviant when cast on a feminine body. It's almost an inversion of twerking—another dance phenomenon white Americans took some time to fully metabolize. Bucking is done to the bawdy, pulsating fortissimo of a raucous brass section, the crack of a snare, or the explosive boom of a bass drum. Doing so becomes an affirmation that a receptive sexual partner can also claim pleasure by thrusting ecstatically, a rebuff against an American sexual politics that historically resigns the passive partner to demurring sex. Straight black women and gay black bottoms reclaim power through the movement by refuting a white, puritanical dictum that bodies should not desire or enjoy the passive position... though, of course, it's classier than that.

But majorettes achieve something beyond the merely sexual. The showmanship of dance lines owes as much to the tradition of burlesque, the art of the tease raised to the level of theatre. And dance lines achieve their fullest expression when working to physically animate the band's sound, stationed to come alive like dashboard figurines to the sound at their backs, a constant reminder that the band's music is intended not only to be received, but also to animate the crowd. The audience should not only be awed by the spectacle of an auxiliary; majorette dance lines incite the audience to move themselves.

By compromising the rigidity of the marching band's militaristic precision, dance lines remind spectators that within that rigidity, there is still space for all kinds of human expression: the seductive, yes, but also the playful, the joyous, and the ecstatic. This dialectic—between standing at attention or in formation and surrendering to the occasional impulse to exclaim or improvise—is a hallmark of black culture, an echo of the call and response found in its music and style.

The majoretting seen at black colleges has experienced sporadic widespread exposure since the early '70s, mostly due to its proximity to the spectacle of the marching band. In the 1990 televised Motown retrospective *Motown 30*, Jackson State University's band, The Sonic Boom of the South, and its J-Settes marched and performed at the Pantages Theatre. Since 1991, NBC Sports has broadcast the Bayou Classic, offering a national audience glimpses of the sequined majorettes of Southern and Grambling State. In 2003, JSU again took the stage for a televised event, this time the

NAACP Image Awards. But due to the rising popularity of commercial dance, majoretting has begun to attract admirers singularly interested in its artistry.

The rise of a different squad of Dancing Dolls, the youth competitive dance team formed by veteran dancer Dianna Williams in Jackson, Mississippi, in 2010, has ignited interest in the discipline in young girls nationally, especially throughout the Southeastern states. (This group has no affiliation with Southern University's Dancing Dolls.) Though not a former J-Sette or SU Dancing Doll herself, Williams began training as a dancer as a child and started the Grove Park Dancerettes in 2002, also serving as a recreational aide and dance instructor in north Jackson. Since 2014, she's been the star of Lifetime's *Bring It!*, which records the lives of the Dancing Dolls and the sometimes-volatile relationship between Williams and the girls' stage moms. The team has enjoyed enough success that it has been franchised in both Birmingham, Alabama, and Atlanta, Georgia. In June 2019, *Bring It! Live*, a road show featuring dancers from the series, embarked on its fourth touring season, generating further widespread interest in the form.

Lifetime combined the elements of a traditional reality show with captivating performance footage in its production of *Bring It!* Despite the shouting matches outside the dance studio or emotional breakdowns from dancers backstage, the results of Williams' tough love methods proved successful, as girls as young as four executed routines. Alums of the show have gone on to audition and perform as members of traditional black college dance lines once they've enrolled as students, proof that dance instructors are successfully constructing a pipeline into the collegiate ranks. This past season, Janae Harrington, formerly of Lifetime's *Step It Up* reality program, danced with Alabama State University as captain of the Stingette dance line; and former Dancing Dolls of Jackson and *Bring It!* stars Camryn Harris and Makalah Whisenton performed weekly as members of the Southern University Dancing Dolls and Jackson State University J-Settes, respectively.

Amateur videographers who formerly recorded the entire band now limit their focus exclusively to the dance lines. These videos now serve as an impressive library documenting the dance genre. Stand counts were once passed down solely through collective memory. They're now being preserved on film. Amateur filmmakers like Trinion Winbush, Marvin Price, and Demaridge have all meticulously compiled footage of collegiate dance lines as far back as 2011 on YouTube channels of the form, making the dances available to watch more broadly.

Price and Winbush have even broadened their catalogs to include lifestyle and performance videos of the McKinley Pantherettes, an accomplished high school majorette line in Baton Rouge, Louisiana, who regularly supplies dancers to the SU Dancing Doll ranks.

These YouTube channels also increase the visibility of gay male and gender-nonconforming majorettes in the South. Traditionally, a clandestine alliance has existed between the all-women teams and their ardent gay admirers. Southern piety dictated that queer performers be relegated to serving as coaches, choreographers, or spectators in the conservatively gendered spaces where college dance lines performed. But largely through collaborations between choreographer Kentrell Collins and dance lines throughout the SWAC, HBCU dance lines now offer instruction and affirmation to aspiring male and female majorette dancers. Collins and The Prancing Elites, a gay and gender-nonconforming dance team from Mobile, Alabama, even appeared on Oxygen's *The Prancing Elite Project* for two seasons. He's since begun organizing the biannual HBCU Dance Affair, a rare opportunity for Southern black gay men and straight black women to come together as allies in celebrating femininity.

Since the release of Beyoncé's *Homecoming*, the visibility of black college majorettes has only grown. In December 2019, rapper Lizzo, TIME Magazine's Entertainer of the Year, featured the Southern University Dancing Dolls, along with the entire SU Human Jukebox Marching Band, in the video for her hit single "Good as Hell". The Season 3 promo for Freeform TV's *grown-ish* also included dancers marching in the style of black college majorettes.

Majorettes from Grambling State University, known as the Orchesis Dance Company, film *Taking the Stands*, a reality TV-style show for YouTube. In 2019, they performed for Beyoncé at an event celebrating her Netflix documentary, released one year after the Beychella performance.

I've been watching majorette videos on YouTube since 2012. Watching these videos in adulthood made me feel proud (as someone throwing a hip to the beat of a bass drum is wont to do), knowing that this artistry is so deeply embedded in black American life, there was little danger of it ever being appropriated. It was mine, something of home to unwrap, no matter how far I'd traveled from my Southern roots. The brassy sound of the band from my computer speakers was not unlike how it felt to walk beneath the stands at a stadium for a black college classic as a child, holding the hand of my father, my cousin LaTeisha, my cousin Rita. Even as a grown man, that choreography and sound gave me access to parts of myself both private and dear— Southern, black, sissy, somebody's child.

The art form is still mine, intimately so, in the way much black art remains. It's just that now the world knows about it. Hopefully, future generations will too. ◉

Pass

Toni Jensen

AFTER OUR LAST CLASS, SHE TELLS ME. OUR ROOM for the graduate seminar is nearly windowless, cinder-block, small. We sit near the corner, in our ridiculous desk-chair combos. After the last of her classmates say their goodbyes, we get to it: one of her undergraduate students has accused her of showing up to teach her class drunk. She's leaving the university, she says. She can't take any more. She can't. It's a last-straw sort of situation.

This woman, I'll call her Marie, is one of the few students of color in our MFA program. She's a talented writer; a steady, intelligent presence in her classes.

As a graduate teaching assistant, she's been bullied by some undergraduates in one previous class. They accused her of being incompetent. Though none were particularly specific, though none came forward to speak to her directly or to levy any direct, specific charge, the department began a file. There were meetings. There was no conversation about race, about the confluence of race and gender, unless the student was the one talking.

In the class, this semester, though, the one containing the drunk-talk student, all has been well. We're in the last week of the semester when the complaint arrives alongside the spring rain. The department will add this to her file. She may have to go on probation.

"Is everyone passing the class?" I ask.

She shakes her head.

"Did they ask you that?"

Another head shake.

No one outside this small, nearly windowless, cinderblock room is talking about the accuser's potential motivations. No one is talking about how Marie doesn't drink. No one is talking about where we live—Arkansas, which some say is where the Midwest meets the South. I would say we're Midwestern in how we don't, as a culture, as a practice, talk straight if we talk at all. I would say we're Southern in how the last thing we're good at is holding meaningful conversations about race.

When I say, repeatedly, "You don't even drink,"

Marie laughs the kind of laugh that is a last laugh, an all-finished laugh.

"It's so insulting," she says.

I say to my student that I both know what she's going through and that I don't. "You can pass," she says, nodding.

From my slumped position in my desk-chair combo, my head swivels, and then I nod. It's true. I'm Métis, I'm Native, but I absolutely can pass.

There isn't much to say, after. Outside, in the dark and damp, we hug and shake off some of the seriousness, and we laugh a little because, what else? I watch her turn right, and I turn left, toward my car, and the rain shifts from hard, straight, and steady to intermittent, to the kind that comes toward you at all angles.

I drive down M.L.K. Jr. Boulevard toward home. This street, which borders the Southern edge of campus, also is known as the Trail of Tears. The historic marker two blocks from my house will let you know where you are if you didn't before. It's good sometimes to be reminded, even if the reminder leaves you holding in your breath a beat too long. It's good sometimes to have the impulse toward forgetting and then to be reminded of the literal—where you are—with the past made present, with it carried and lived as you drive on home.

. . .

When I was a graduate student in Texas, the first time I brought a story into workshop, a fellow student told me if I was going to "write about Indians," I would need to separate my writing more from that of Louise Erdrich. Then this man misquoted from the beginning of Erdrich's novel *Tracks*, ostensibly to show how similar it was to my story. At the end of workshop when it was my turn to speak, I corrected his misquotation and suggested in my most polite voice that perhaps to him "Indians" writing about snow all seemed the same. I assured him we were not. I assured him, though we might both have written about snow, neither of us was "writing about Indians."

I made two friends that day, a Black woman and the white, Republican son of a wealthy Texas oil family. I learned fast that I would be surprised in this place by who would be good company. The class held mostly white, female faces, and not one of those women looked me in the eye or spoke to me, then or after.

Later, more company arrived—queer writers and Latino and Chicano writers and another Native writer—so I had far more company than did Marie, far more voices pushing alongside mine.

We needed each other. Another white, male student wrote as his comment on one of my poems, "Stop writing the in for the moment but sure not to last Indian poems." What I was writing, it seemed, was considered a fad, temporary, "sure not to last." I was writing my life. So I then was temporary, a fad, "sure not to last." How can you stay in a place if your very existence is "sure not to last"? If not for my company, I might have believed him. If not for my company, I would not have stayed. It would have been a last-straw moment.

When a white male student in workshop started writing stories using all of us as recognizable characters, when he made the character that was me get run over by a Ford Escort, my company took me to the bar and bought drink after drink after drink. After, they called me "Ford Escort" in the halls. They maybe said it too loud because the next story from this writer was a different sort of story, a domestic violence sort of story, featuring my character tied to a chair, a man holding a gun to her head.

The land on which that university sits was for so many years fought over and lived on by Apache and Comanche people, who still live there, of course, just not in such numbers. We were all of us visitors. We were all of us invaders—though some more than others.

"Why—" my friend Marcus asked in that workshop, "why do you think you can do that to her?"

"It's a character," said another white man.

The writer's laugh was not believable as humor or comedy, and it went on much too long. I felt such anger but also a little sorry for him, for how long everyone held the silence, after.

. . .

I've been a student or a teacher for so many years in this region we call the South. I've worked so hard to make the four walls of my classroom a place where all the Maries are welcome, where all the Marcuses know they can ask the question, where all conversations are possible, where everyone knows where we are—the limitations of it, alongside the possibilities.

In my neighborhood, just off the Trail of Tears, the day after the last day of class, I walk the dogs around the block to see if we're flooding, to see whose yards or houses have taken on water. That's how I think of it now, this place—a *we* rather than an *it*. I've acclimated far enough to feel a measure of belonging.

But how much of that is on account of my ability to pass? How much grace is it possible to give others when you move through the world with more than a small measure of safety—when this is safety you own but have not bought?

Where my family is from, where the Métis are from in Canada, we were once known as "Road Allowance People." Between 1885 and 1945, Métis got the name when the Canadian government decided to dissolve our land base, to sell 160 acres for $160 through scrip certificates, which were easy enough to forge or transfer, which were often forged or transferred through impersonation. If Métis sometimes could pass for white, whites could sometimes pass for Métis. They could sometimes steal our land through this passing.

Without a land base, some Métis became squatters on our own land, became Road Allowance People.

We lived in shacks made from logs or leftover lumber, covered rough with tarpaper. We lived like this through prairie winters.

Back in my neighborhood, the water has flooded the street and the sidewalk. The dogs and I round the corner. Across the field a crow pecks at a full, intact pineapple washed up through the drainage system and landed here at the intersection. A neighbor pushes mud from her sidewalk with a wide broom across the street and into the drainage opening by my yard. "There's mud on the sidewalk," she says, shaking her head, but no word on the pineapple lying a few yards behind her.

I know the South is not the only place capable of irony, capable of rough treatment, of racism and worse. I know I have spent so much time considering the safety of my students within my classroom walls, but I have not considered enough the limitations of this place, of this South, of this history, outside my classroom walls, outside my own defining of it.

I know my own passing to be a complicated crossing. ◉

Gum

Diana Cejas

IT STICKS TO EVERYTHING. STAINS YOUR SKIN, cakes under your nails and makes them crack or tear or bleed. Cleaning yourself hardly helps. You scrub long enough and the grime might wash away but the odor lingers. Sun-ripened raspberry and honey vanilla soaps can't quite cover it up. It stays with you. A year might go by, a decade. You get caught in a cloud of cigarette smoke one day and you inhale and there it is. Motor oil and tractor exhaust. The sun beating down on red clay fields. You in rubber boots, thick pants, and a hat, sweating, swearing, standing among rows and rows of tobacco. The brown gum covering its yellow-green leaves. The brown gum smeared all over your hands. I still smell it in my sleep.

Every spring, summer, and fall from my sixth birthday to the day that I packed up and left for college revolved around tobacco. It was the same for my mother and her mother and hers. My family could mark the passage of time by matching it to the growing cycle. I lost my first tooth shortly after my grandfather sewed seeds into frost-kissed earth. I got my first period the evening after a morning spent on the planter, the rusted metal seat staining my clothes. Every cycle was the same. I woke up, got dressed, went to school, came back, went to the fields, wished for winter to come. Every day was the same.

The only thing that got me out of the fields, aside from the period, was schoolwork. My grandmother worked as a teacher's aide when she wasn't working on the farm. She expected excellence. Sometimes I'd bring my books to the fields. I'd work through math problems while sitting in my grandfather's rickety pickup truck. Switch with my sister when it was my turn to prime the leaves and her turn to do worksheets. Sometimes I turned in papers that were sprinkled with dusty red clay. I live on a tobacco farm, I'd say if anybody asked. Their eyebrows would lift a little. They always looked surprised. Little black girls don't live on farms anymore, I guess. It's algebra two, I'd say if anybody asked. For some reason, the looks that I got were the same.

As I grew, I wanted less to do with fertilizer and plows and spent more time on my assignments. I got bigger. I could snap the pink and white flowers from the top of the tallest stalks. I started a project on photosynthesis. I got stronger. My cousins and I piled brightleaf on burlap and heaved the giant sacs onto trailers. I toted thick textbooks home from school every day. I applied to college. Of course I did. I got good grades. I had more options than just the fields and Liggett factories. I left before the harvest. My grandfather watched me go. Tears in his eyes and mud on his boots and tobacco gum underneath his nails. My grandmother watched me go. She looked less sad than determined.

It is strange to go into the healing business all the while knowing that the thing that has killed so many people is the thing that fed you, clothed you, got you to school. I sat in biology classes, learned about what tobacco does to you, saw blackened lungs and cancerous mouths. I stopped saying that I lived on a tobacco farm. I left that part out, let my roommates imagine dairy cows and bright red barns. My mother sent care packages after the auctions ended and all of the money had come in. Each cardboard box was full of snacks and sweets and smelled like old pine walls and sunbaked earth and dried leaves and burlap and home. I filled my belly and choked a little on my lies.

I got older. My grandparents did too. It got harder for my grandfather to climb high up in the tobacco barn and fill the rafters with leaf-laden sticks. My grandmother got arthritis. Each knuckle creaked and curled. She stopped working. She grew tomatoes instead. When I was eighteen, they took the buyout. That was smart, wasn't it? To keep your land and be paid not to grow. To move away from tobacco and help usher in a healthy new age for North Carolina. Smoke-free. My grandfather never did smoke. My grandmother quit in her youth. My grandfather quit going to the Farm Bureau and auctions and warehouses. Didn't see Roger or Leroy or any of the other farmers, the workers, the people he had known since my mother was a girl. Didn't see them for a while. My grandmother didn't stop going to church. She didn't talk about the harvest. She told Miss Irene, Miss Melba, and Miss Alease about how well my sister and I were doing in school.

At some point, farming became fashionable. I grew up on a farm, I'd say if anybody asked. My colleagues' eyebrows would lift a little. They'd tell me about sustainable practices and backyard chicken coops. They'd tell me about homesteading and potager gardens and Pinterest. You don't know anything, I wanted to say. I grew up on a farm. I grew up with tobacco in my hands and red clay beneath my feet and Carolina blue skies above me and that means something. The white couple that moved into the house where my schoolmates used to play grew a patch of greenwood tobacco in their front yard. For decoration, they'd say. Heirloom seeds. I'd say nothing.

I wrote a report in graduate school about green tobacco sickness. It took me sixty-five-hundred words and a poster presentation to say that a plant that can kill you from the inside out can also kill you from the outside in. Or at least give you a nasty headache. I scanned medical textbooks, saw pictures of men who looked like my grandfather standing in rubber boots, thick pants, and hats. The symptoms are worse when the skin is wet. I pictured him on the tractor, sweat sticking his shirt to his skin. I tried to remember if he had ever been nauseous or crampy or weak. All I could remember was the scalding metal seat, the mud on his hands, the splinters in my hands from hoisting tobacco sticks loaded down with fresh leaves over to him. Some splinters he removed with his knife. I got an A on the report.

At some point, it occurred to me that I wanted to go home. I'd said that I would never go back. I'd promised Mama that I would always go back. I spent eighteen years getting one degree and then the next and the next. I lived in cities so big you couldn't see stars in the sky. Went to libraries big enough to get lost in. I thought that was what I wanted. One day I got caught up in a cloud of cigarette smoke. I inhaled and there it was. The sweat on my skin and the ache in my back and the gum on my hands and the place that I am from. And there I was. ◉

Contributors

JASWINDER BOLINA is an American poet and essayist. His books include, *The 44th of July*, *Phantom Camera*, *Carrier Wave*, and the digital chapbook *The Tallest Building in America*. His poems have appeared in numerous literary journals and been included in *The Best American Poetry* series. His essays can be found at *The Poetry Foundation*, *McSweeney's*, *Himal Southasian*, *The Writer*, and other magazines. He teaches on the faculty of the MFA Program in Creative Writing at the University of Miami.

DR. REGINA N. BRADLEY is a writer and researcher of African American Life and Culture with an emphasis on the contemporary American South. She is the Assistant Professor of English and African Diaspora Studies at Kennesaw State University in Kennesaw, Georgia. Dr. Bradley is the author of the forthcoming book *Chronicling Stankonia: OutKast and the Rise of the Hip Hop South* and editor of the forthcoming *An OutKast Reader*.

DIANA CEJAS is a pediatric neurologist and writer in Durham, North Carolina. Her essays and opinion pieces have appeared in medical publications including the Journal of the American Medical Association and Neurology. Works of creative nonfiction and short stories have appeared or are forthcoming in *Catapult, Passages North, The Dead Mule School of Southern Literature* and others.

JENNIFER HOPE CHOI is the recipient of the Carson McCullers Center's Marguerite and Lamar Smith Fellowship, the BuzzFeed Emerging Writer Fellowship, and a 2019 Pushcart Prize Special Mention. She is also a Bread Loaf scholar and an Aspen Words fellow. Her writing has appeared in *Virginia Quarterly Review, Guernica, The American Scholar, Bon Appétit, Lucky Peach, BuzzFeed Reader, The Atlantic*, and elsewhere.

TIANA CLARK is the author of the poetry collection, *I Can't Talk About the Trees Without the Blood* and *Equilibrium.* Clark is a winner of the 2020 Kate Tufts Discovery Award, and a 2019 National Endowment for the Arts Literature Fellow. Her writing has appeared in or is forthcoming from *The New Yorker, Poetry Magazine, The Washington Post, VQR, Tin House Online, Kenyon Review, BuzzFeed News, American Poetry Review, New England Review, Oxford American, Best New Poets 2015*, and elsewhere. She teaches creative writing at Southern Illinois University at Edwardsville.

CHRISTENA CLEVELAND Ph.D. is a social psychologist, public theologian, author, and activist. She is the founder and director of the recently-launched Center for Justice +

Renewal. Dr. Cleveland holds a Ph.D. in social psychology from the University of California Santa Barbara as well as an honorary doctorate from the Virginia Theological Seminary. Dr. Cleveland is based in North Carolina where she lives with her spouse, Jim.

OSAYI ENDOLYN is a James Beard Award winner whose work reflects on food, culture and identity. Her writing appears in *Time, the Washington Post, the Los Angeles Times, the Wall Street Journal, Eater, Food & Wine* and *the Oxford American.* She's been featured on *Chef's Table* and *Ugly Delicious* on Netflix, *the Sporkful, Special Sauce with Ed Levine*, 1A, and *The Splendid Table.* She was awarded the UC Berkeley-11th Hour Food and Farming Journalism Fellowship. She's working on several forthcoming book projects.

M. EVELINA GALANG has been named one of the 100 most influential Filipinas in the United States and at-large by the Filipina Women's Network. She is the author of the story collection *Her Wild American Self*, novels *One Tribe*, and *Angel de la Luna and the 5th Glorious Mystery*, and nonfiction *Lola's House: Filipino Women Living with War.*

LATRIA GRAHAM is a journalist, cultural critic, and fifth generation South Carolina farmer. She is a graduate of Dartmouth College, and later earned her MFA in Creative Nonfiction from The New School in New York City. Her work has been featured in the *New York Times*, the *Los Angeles Times*, the *Guardian, Southern Living*, and *Garden & Gun.*

MINDA HONEY's writing has been featured in the *Los Angeles Review of Books, the Washington Post, the Guardian, the Oxford American, Teen Vogue*, and every other week she tackles the dating woes of strangers as her city's relationship advice columnist at the *LEO Weekly*. Minda lives in Louisville, Kentucky where she serves as the Director of the BFA in Creative Writing program at Spalding University.

GARY JACKSON is the author of the poetry collection *Missing You, Metropolis*, which received the 2009 Cave Canem Poetry Prize. His poems have appeared in numerous journals including *Callaloo, Tin House, Los Angeles Review of Books*, and *Crab Orchard Review*. He was featured in the 2013 New American Poetry Series by the Poetry Society of America and is the recipient of both a Cave Canem and Bread Loaf fellowship. He is an associate professor at the College of Charleston and is the associate poetry editor at *Crazyhorse*.

TONI JENSEN is the author of *Carry*, a memoir-in-essays about gun violence, and a short story collection, *From the Hilltop*. She is the recipient of a National Endowment for the Arts Literature Fellowship for 2020. Her essays and stories have been published in journals such as *Orion, Catapult* and *Ecotone*. She teaches in the Programs in Creative Writing and Translation at the University of Arkansas and in the low residency MFA Program at the Institute of American Indian Arts. She is Métis.

SONIAH KAMAL is a novelist, essayist and public speaker. Her most recent novel, *Unmarriageable*, is a 2019 *Financial*

Times Readers' Best Book, a 2019 "Book All Georgians Should Read", a 2020 Georgia Author of the Year for Literary Fiction nominee, and is shortlisted for the 2020 Townsend Prize for Fiction. Her critically acclaimed debut novel, *An Isolated Incident*, was shortlisted for several prizes. Soniah's work is in the *New York Times, The Guardian, Buzzfeed, Georgia Review, Catapult, Normal School, The Bitter Southerner*, and more.

ARUNI KASHYAP is the author of the novel *The House With a Thousand Stories*. His short stories, poems and essays have appeared or are forthcoming in *The Oxford Anthology of Writings from Northeast, The Kenyon Review, The New York Times, The Guardian UK, the Hindu, Evergreen Review, Karthika Review, Juked, Sin Fronteras Journal, Stonecoast Review, The Atticus Review*, and others. He is an Assistant Professor of Creative Writing at University of Georgia, Athens.

DEVI S. LASKAR's debut novel, *The Atlas of Reds and Blues* has garnered praise in *The Washington Post, Chicago Review of Books, Booklist*. She holds an MFA from Columbia University and an MA from The University of Illinois. Her work has appeared or is forthcoming from such journals as *Rattle, Tin House and Crab Orchard Review*. A native of Chapel Hill, North Carolina, she now lives in California.

KIESE LAYMON is a black Southern writer, born and raised in Jackson, Mississippi. He earned an MFA in Fiction from Indiana University. Laymon is currently the Ottilie Schillig Professor of English and Creative Writing at the University of Mississippi. Laymon is the author of the novel, *Long Division,* a collection of essays, *How to Slowly Kill Yourself and Others in America*, and *Heavy: An American Memoir. Heavy* was named one of the Best Books of 2018 by outlets including the *New York Times, NPR, the Washington Post*, and many more. Laymon has written essays, stories and reviews for the *New York Times, NPR, LitHub*, the *Los Angeles Times,* the *Guardian, Oxford American, Vanity Fair*, the *Paris Review*, among others.

FREDERICK MCKINDRA, fiction writer and essayist, lives in Little Rock, Arkansas. He attended Howard University and holds an MFA in Fiction Writing from the New School. His essay "Becoming Integrated" from the Fall 2017 issue of the *Oxford American* was listed as a Notable Essay in *Best American Essays 2018*. He also contributed a monthly column throughout 2018 to the *OA*'s online series "The By and By." A 2017 Buzzfeed Emerging Writer Fellow, Frederick has received support from the Bread Loaf Writer's Conference as a 2017 Work Study Scholarship Recipient for Fiction and the Lambda Literary Foundation as a 2016 Fiction Fellow.

NICHOLE PERKINS is a writer from Nashville, Tennessee, currently living in Brooklyn. Her work frequently covers the intersections of pop culture, race, sex, gender, and relationships. She co-hosts *Thirst Aid Kit*, a podcast about pop culture, desire, and the female gaze, and *The Waves*, a podcast that looks at news and culture through a feminist lens. Her first collection of poetry, *Lilith, But Dark*, was published by Publishing Genius in 2018.

JOY PRIEST is the author of *Horsepower*, winner of the Donald Hall Prize for Poetry. Her poems and essays appear in numerous publications, including ESPN, *Gulf Coast, Mississippi Review, the Rumpus*, and *Virginia Quarterly Review*. She is a PhD candidate in Creative Writing & Literature at the University of Houston.

IVELISSE RODRIGUEZ's debut short story collection *Love War Stories* is a 2019 PEN/Faulkner finalist and a 2018 Foreword Reviews INDIES finalist. She has published fiction in the *Boston Review, All about Skin: Short Fiction by Women of Color, Obsidian, Kweli, the Bilingual Review, Aster(ix)*, and other publications. She was a senior fiction editor at *Kweli* and is a Kimbilio Fellow and a VONA/ Voices alum. She earned an MFA in Creative Writing from Emerson College and a PhD in English-Creative Writing from the University of Illinois at Chicago.

NATALIA SYLVESTER is the author of two novels for adults, *Chasing the Sun* and *Everyone Knows You Go Home*, which won an International Latino Book Award and the Jesse H. Jones Award for Best Work of Fiction from the Texas Institute of Letters. *Running*, her debut novel for young adults, is a 2020 Junior Library Guild Selection. Born in Lima, Peru, Sylvester grew up in Florida and Texas and received a BFA in Creative Writing from the University of Miami. Her essays have appeared in the *New York Times, Bustle, Catapult, Electric Literature, Latina Magazine, McSweeney's*, and the *Austin American-Statesman*. ◉

Notes

The following essays have been previously published:

"A New Normal South: Southern Cooking By Indian American Chefs Offers Refreshing Ways To Connect," in *Gravy*; "That's Not Actually True" in *Scalawag*; "The Rich, Southern History of Black College Majorettes" in *BuzzFeed*; a variation of "Face" in the *New York Times*. ◉

A Note on the Cover Artist

JOHN MATA is an illustrator and designer located in Dallas, Texas, whose work has appeared on and in NPR, Herb Lester, ESPN, *The Washington Post* BrandStudio, and more.

He is currently an Art Director for Panini America; designing trading cards for the NFL and NBA. He's also obsessed with vintage space travel.

Freelance inquiries: johnmata@eight-zero.com. ◉

A Note on Book Sales Proceeds

To support racial justice and equitability in the South, contributors to this anthology, along with its editor, have donated their writer and editor fees to the Southern Poverty Law Center, a non profit legal advocacy group dedicated to fighting hate and bigotry and to seeking justice for the most vulnerable members of our society.

The SPLC was founded in 1971 to ensure that the promise of the civil rights movement became a reality for all. Since then, its lawyers have won numerous landmark legal victories on behalf of the exploited, the powerless, and the forgotten.

The SPLC is a catalyst for racial justice in the South and beyond, working in partnership with communities to dismantle white supremacy, strengthen intersectional movements, and advance the human rights of all people. ◉

PUBLISHING
New & Extraordinary
VOICES FROM THE
AMERICAN SOUTH

HUB CITY PRESS is the leading independent publisher of Southern literature. Focused on finding and spotlighting new and extraordinary voices from the American South, the press has published over one hundred high-caliber literary works. Hub City is interested in books with a strong sense of place and is committed to introducing a diverse roster of lesser-heard voices. We are funded by the National Endowment for the Arts, Amazon Literary Partnership, the South Carolina Arts Commission and hundreds of donors across the Carolinas.

Hub City Press gratefully acknowledges support from the National Endowment for the Arts, the Amazon Literary Partnership, South Carolina Arts Commission, the, Chapman Cultural Center in Spartanburg, South Carolina, and Mr. and Mrs. George Dean Johnson Jr.

TEXT Sabon MT Pro 11/15.5
DISPLAY Frank New 16/20